Walter Pedrotti

101 *traditional recipes for*

SPAGHETTI

Venice, Italy,
November 2000

Fran Hahm

Edizioni LA LIBRERIA DI DEMETRA

Editing: Paola Turrini
Translation: Studio Labor
Layout: Ilaria Stradiotti
Photography: Arc-en-ciel (Verona).

*For Riccardo and Titti
who make the best
spaghetti with anchovies
that I've ever eaten*

101 TRADITIONAL RECIPES FOR **SPAGHETTI**
2nd edition july 1998
© DEMETRA S.r.l.
Via Strà, 167 – S.S. 11
37030 Colognola ai Colli (VR)
Tel. 045/6174111 - Fax 045/6174100

The powerful P3 lodge

There is no doubt that wheat has been the staple food of most of the worlds population for a very long time, Europeans included. In fact, despite the general drop in its consumption, which goes hand in hand with that of other cereals, it is still of very significant importance, above all in Mediterranean countries, a fact which is amply demonstrated by the diffusion of the powerful and distinct "P3 Lodge" – pane, pasta, pizza (i.e. bread, pasta, pizza). In Italy, in particular, bread, pasta and pizza are present in almost every meal, in one way or another, they are the foundations of "a good meal", or at least they accompany it. Just think about pasta: how many kinds are there? And how many ways are there of serving it? It is even difficult to attempt to take a census... For the Italians, in particular, pasta is a faithful, lifelong companion and spaghetti more so than other pastas. In short, we can say, without fear of exaggerating, that we owe our civilisation to wheat.

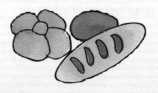

Wheat

Wheat (or grain) is generally classed as soft or durum. Soft wheat is currently the most diffused and constitutes the best part of the cereal used for breadmaking; in Italy it is cultivated mainly in the central regions and the north.

Durum wheat is less diffused because it needs hot, dry climates to grow. In Italy it is cultivated in the south and on the islands, and is used in the preparation of pasta: it is rich in gluten which is a particular mix of proteins.

The grain of wheat, when ground, provides us with flour, it is made up of different layers, like all the other cereals.

Some of these layers are eliminated during refinement and, depending on the type of grinding, different things can be obtained from the seed.

In the case of flour, a more or less refined product is obtained, so there are several grades of flour; 00, 0, 1, 2 and wholewheat. In the less refined flours there is a higher percentage of raw fibre, as well as other elements like trace elements and vitamins, that are mainly found in the external layer of the caryosis.

Two essential requirements for good spaghetti

Good spaghetti, the pride of Mediterranean cuisine, must have at least two essential qualities.

Firstly, it must not overcook too quickly, this is guaranteed by the use of durum wheat, whilst the use of soft wheat means that the pasta becomes sticky as soon as it reaches, or goes slightly over, the recommended cooking time.

So the general rule is not to use soft wheat, but bad quality pastas are certainly not rare. Secondly spaghetti, and all pasta in general, must have a characteristic taste: a good pasta isn't just a base for a sauce, but must have a distinct flavour.

Pastas which are dried slowly are particularly tasty, sometimes they are dried for more than 12 hours, a process which triggers fermentation and gives the pasta its own particular flavour.

How to cook spaghetti

Good spaghetti must be well cooked but "al dente". So here are some simple rules which should be followed carefully:

• use 1 litre of water for every 100 g of pasta, add 10 g of salt when the water begins to boil;

- put the pasta in the water only when it is boiling;
- stir often, with a wooden spoon, whilst cooking, so that the pasta does not become too sticky with the starch that is released into the water;
- drain and serve the pasta as soon as it reaches the recommended cooking time.

Wholewheat Spaghetti

Spaghetti made with wholewheat flour, besides being characterised by its darker colour, also has quite a different taste to spaghetti made with refined flour. Without doubt it is more filling and in many ways preferable to "white" spaghetti, it is ideal with vegetable based sauces.

In the following recipes you can, if you like, use wholewheat pasta instead of "white" pasta. Its cooking needs no special precautions, or complicated and exotic preparation.

Oil

After years in which, particularly in some countries with faster economic development, the use of olive oil seemed to have been supplanted by the much publicised use of oils of various sorts of seeds that boasted exceptional nutritional characteristics, olive oil has recently made a great comeback to our dining tables.

In fact, today, it is recommended by nutritionists and dieticians, and by other institutions that safeguard our health, they indicate that it is the best fat to use in pregnancy, for children and for the elderly.

Certainly in Italy, which is one of the primary producers of olive oil in the world, it has always been highly valued and never ceased to be favoured by a large segment of consumers.

So it is no surprise that the consumption of this oil and, particularly, of extra virgin olive oil. Obtained by cold pressing the olives, is said to have important benefits.

Research has been done that demonstrates that consumption lowers the number of various cardiovascular illnesses: it has recently been established, for instance, that in northern countries, where fats of animal origin are widely used (butter, lard, suet etc.), the number of people suffering from cardiovascular illnesses is four to five times greater than in the countries of the

Mediterranean basin, in which the consumption of olive oil has remained at significant levels.

We must consider, then, that the attention dedicated in recent years to diet has allowed a revaluation of some of the typical foods of our tradition, which, if we look closely, are almost always of vegetable origin, a picture emerges in which olive oil is given much more importance. In the so-called Mediterranean diet it accompanies cereals – pasta in particular – vegetables and pulses, the various benefits of these foods have been emphasised, as they are tied to a simpler way of eating, instead of that to which we have become accustomed in the recent decades of widespread economic comfort.

Olive oil is, therefore, one of the traditional foods of our civilisation, and so could not avoid attracting the attention of medics, dieticians and nutritionists, always attentive, amongst other things, to the fact that this food of ancient origin has survived for so long and largely maintained its identity and genuineness, particularly in the case of the cold pressed oil, whose production cycle has undergone very few changes over the course of centuries.

The cold processing of olives, the extraction by simple pressure, without heating the pulp of the olives and without the addition of water to the pulp itself or to the oily must, in fact gives the extra virgin olive oil a bio-nutritional and organoleptic superiority and makes it easier to preserve than other oils. In particular cold pressing safeguards the principles, which are composed of phenolic and volatile aromatic substances, responsible for the aroma of the oil. Extra virgin olive oil is, by the way, the most heat resistant oil (cooking and frying) and, despite what is often thought, it is also the most digestible.

It should, however, preferably be consumed uncooked, in order to benefit from all its properties. In the recipes that follow, therefore, we always recommend the use of this oil.

Salt

As far as salt is concerned, essential ingredient in the preparation of pasta, it is better to use unrefined sea salt. There are many elements present in this salt which are eliminated during refinement: chloride, sodium, magnesium, sulphur, calcium, potassium, bromine, carbon, zinc, strontium, boron, silica, fluoride, lithium, phosphorus, iodine, arsenic, copper etc. Unrefined rock salt can be found on sale through a government monopoly system, at a controlled price; unrefined table salt can easily be found in specialist food shops and health food shops. In the recipes which follow, for salt we intend unrefined sea salt.

Quick recipes

We are in an era in which time never seems to be enough and, even when cooking, we have to watch the clock. But instead of giving up the pleasures of good eating we can find a way to brighten up the dinner table with simple creations, rich in flavour and fantasy, which allow us to transform the most humble plate of spaghetti into something tasty and appetising.

• Plain spaghetti - 1 •

400 g of spaghetti, salt, 3 cloves of garlic,
7 dessert spoons of extra virgin olive oil.

This is a very simple way to prepare and season spaghetti. It is particularly suitable for when you have very little time available or when you are surprised by unexpected guests: oil and garlic are usually available in any kitchen.

First put the spaghetti on to cook in plenty of boiling, salted water, in the meantime take a large serving dish and rub a crushed clove of garlic around the edge.

Crush the rest of the garlic and place it in the bottom of the dish with the olive oil. When the pasta is al dente drain it and add it to the oil in the dish, add a little more oil and mix thoroughly so that the heat from the spaghetti releases the aroma of the seasoning. Serve immediately.

• Plain spaghetti - 2 •

400 g of spaghetti, salt, 5 medium size ripe tomatoes,
2 cloves of garlic, a few leaves of fresh basil, a pinch of pepper,
7 dessert spoons of extra virgin olive oil.

An easy to prepare summer dish, characterised by the full flavour of ripe tomatoes and the aroma of fresh basil, it cannot fail to meet with the approval of your guests. Wash, dry and roughly chop the tomatoes, crush the garlic and chop the basil, place them in a serving dish with the oil. Leave everything to soak for about 1/2 of an hour in a cool place. In the meantime put the water for the spaghetti on, when it begins to boil add some salt and the spaghetti. When al dente, drain the spaghetti and pour it into the serving dish, add a pinch of pepper and salt if necessary, stir well before serving.

• Tricolour spaghetti •

*400 g of spaghetti, salt, 400 g of ripe tomatoes,
150 g fresh mozzarella cheese, a few leaves of fresh basil,
oregano, 1 dessert spoon of salted capers, grated parmesan cheese,
extra virgin olive oil (about 7 dessert spoons)*

This is a very quick and simple, yet tasty, way of preparing and serving spaghetti. Pour the oil into a serving dish, wash, dry and chop the tomatoes and add to the oil, add a good pinch of oregano, a few chopped basil leaves, a pinch of salt and pepper, the rinsed capers and a few spoons of grated parmesan. Then leave the mixture in a cool place for a couple of hours. Put the water on for the spaghetti and when it is boiling add the pasta. When the spaghetti is al dente, drain it and pour it into the serving dish, add the diced mozzarella and then stir thoroughly so that the heat from the pasta melts the mozzarella, serve immediately.

• Classic spaghetti
with garlic and oil •

*400 g of spaghetti, salt, 4 cloves of garlic,
a few sprigs of parsley, pepper, about 1/2 a glass
of extra virgin olive oil.*

The combination of garlic and oil is one of the classic,
quick and easy ways of serving any pasta, not only
spaghetti. Crush the garlic in a frying pan and add the oil,
sauté the garlic over a moderate heat, stirring with a
wooden spoon, avoid letting the Garlic burn, it should be
golden brown. Just before removing from the heat add the
washed and chopped parsley and a little pepper, preferably
freshly ground. Cook the pasta in plenty of salted, boiling
water and when it is al dente drain it and put it in a serving dish, add the oil and garlic and stir.

• Spaghetti with garlic,
oil and chilli pepper •

*400 g of spaghetti, salt, 4 cloves of garlic, chopped
or powdered chilli pepper, grated pecorino cheese (optional),
extra virgin olive oil.*

Garlic, oil and chilli pepper, here we are with, undoubtedly, one of the most famous, simple and tasty pasta recipes.
Heat the oil in a frying pan with the chopped or powdered

BASIL

There are about 150 known varieties of basil. The plants can easily be grown on a the balcony at home, and it is usually the leaves that are used fresh in cooking although the flowering part of the plant can be used. Certainly in the kitchen basil is used mainly as a flavouring, but it is interesting to note that it is considered as having tonic, antispasmodic, stomachic and intestinal antiseptic properties and phytotherapy prescribes it for internal use in cases of asthenia nervosa, insomnia, gastric cramps, migraine, epilepsy and gout. The fresh, torn leaves can be placed on insect bites and the dried, powdered leaves are used as a treatment against loss of smell due to chronic coryza. To dry the leaves it is necessary to pick them just before the plant flowers completely and lay them out in a cool, ventilated place, in the shade, they should be turned over every so often. Then they should be kept in glass jars, or paper bags, in a dry place.

chilli pepper, when it is very hot add the crushed garlic, let it brown, stirring with a wooden spoon, do not let it burn. Meanwhile cook the spaghetti in plenty of salted, boiling water, when it is al dente drain it and pour it into a serving dish along with the spicy oil. Mix thoroughly, and, if you wish to add a little more flavour to the pasta add a little grated pecorino cheese. If you aren't too keen on chilli pepper you can discard it before adding the oil to the spaghetti, in that case it would be better not to chop the chilli pepper too finely. If you prefer you can put the cooked spaghetti directly into the frying pan with the oil and leave it over a low heat for a couple of minutes, to allow the flavours to mingle. And indeed, considering the fact that the chilli pepper loses some of its important elements when cooked — for example vitamin C, which it is particularly rich in — then you can add it, chopped or powdered just before serving, if you prefer.

• Spaghetti with olives •

*400 g of spaghetti, salt, 400 g of ripe tomatoes,
2 cloves of garlic, a chilli pepper or chilli powder,
100 g of green olives, a few fresh basil leaves, extra virgin olive
oil (about 7 dessert spoons).*

Begin by washing, drying and then slicing the tomatoes, crush the garlic, finely chop the chilli pepper, remove the stones and finely chop the olives, chop the basil and place all of these into a serving dish, add the oil and some salt. Leave in a cool place for a couple of hours.

When you are ready cook the spaghetti in plenty of salted, boiling water and, when it is al dente, drain, pour into the serving dish with the sauce and stir thoroughly, serve immediately.

If you are not too keen on chilli pepper you can just break it into pieces instead of chopping it and then remove it from the oil just before adding it to the spaghetti.

• Spaghetti with curry •

*400 g of spaghetti, salt, 1/4 of a litre of fresh single cream,
1 dessert spoon of curry powder, 1/2 a packet of saffron,
extra virgin olive oil.*

Put the water on for the spaghetti and when it boils add
the salt and then the pasta. Meanwhile heat some oil in a
saucepan, add the curry, the saffron and after a couple of
minutes the cream.
Stir with a wooden spoon and allow to simmer for a few
minutes, put a heat diffuser under the pan if possible.
When the pasta is al dente, drain it and add the curry
sauce, stir thoroughly and then serve.

• Spaghetti with lemon •

*400 g of spaghetti, salt, the juice of 1 lemon, 1 fresh spring
onion, a few sprigs of parsley, pepper, extra virgin olive oil.*

This unusual summery sauce, with lemon, is particularly
suitable with fine delicate spaghetti which have a quicker
cooking time. While the pasta is cooking in plenty of salted, boiling water, prepare a mix with the oil, the washed
and finely sliced spring onion, salt and pepper.
When the pasta is cooked al dente, drain it well then add
a little olive oil, stir and leave to go cold, then pour it into a serving dish, add the oil and spring onion mix, some
chopped parsley and the lemon juice.

SAFFRON

Perhaps the most expensive of all the spices, it is the dried stigmas of the crocus sativus, it is grown in Italy with good results and is used in the preparation of risotto, pasta, cereals and sauces, as well as an ingredient in some very good sweets. It is able to colour a quantity of water thousands of times more than its own weight and it is usually dissolved in hot water or milk to obtain a brilliant yellow colour.

Mix thoroughly and serve. It is very important that the spaghetti is drained thoroughly when al dente, otherwise it may continue to "cook" whilst it is cooling.

• Spaghetti with capers and lemon •

400 g of spaghetti, salt, the rind of 1 lemon,
3 dessert spoons of salted capers, 6 dessert spoons
of extra virgin olive oil, pepper.

This is another summer recipe: simple and tasty, very quick and ideal for anyone who suffers from heartburn. Put the water on for the spaghetti and when it boils add the pasta. In the meantime rinse the capers under running water then chop them finely along with the lemon rind and then dilute everything with the oil.
When the spaghetti is cooked al dente, drain it and pour it into a serving dish, add the sauce and a little freshly

ground pepper, stir thoroughly and serve with a bottle of cold white wine, for example a Pinot grigio.

• Spaghetti with mascarpone •

400 g of spaghetti, salt, 40 g of butter,
100 g of mascarpone, 100 g of fresh ricotta,
4 dessert spoons of grated parmesan cheese, pepper.

Bring plenty of salted water to the boil and cook the spaghetti. Meanwhile prepare the sauce. Soften the butter at room temperature and put it in a bowl, stir with a wooden spoon until it is creamy.

Add the crumbled ricotta, the mascarpone and the grated parmesan. Blend all the ingredients thoroughly, adding a couple of spoonfuls of the pasta water, until you have a soft, creamy sauce.

When the spaghetti is cooked al dente drain it and pour it into a warmed serving dish, add the sauce and stir thoroughly, serve with a glass of cold white wine.

• Quick spaghetti
with asparagus •

400 g of spaghetti, salt, 500 g of thin asparagus,
50 g of butter, 4 dessert spoons of single cream,
4 dessert spoons of grated parmesan cheese,
1 teaspoon of mustard.

First trim and thoroughly wash the asparagus, remove the hard part and cut the tips into 2 or 3 pieces.

Put a pan of salted water on to heat, when it begins to boil cook the asparagus and the spaghetti until the spaghetti is al dente. Meanwhile Allow the butter to soften at room temperature then cut it into small pieces, place in a bowl with the cream, the grated cheese and the mustard.

Blend these ingredients very well until you have a creamy mixture. When the pasta is cooked drain it together with the asparagus, pour both into the serving dish with the cream mixture, stir thoroughly and serve.

• Spaghetti with green peppercorns •

400 g of spaghetti, salt, 1 egg yolk, 3 dessert spoons of cream, 3 dessert spoons of green peppercorns in brine, 40 g of butter, 4 dessert spoons of mature ricotta cheese, grated.

Cook the spaghetti in plenty of salted, boiling water, in the meantime prepare the sauce. Beat the egg yolk in a dish with the cream, a pinch of salt and the peppercorns, which have been drained and squashed with a fork: blend well until you have a smooth mixture.

When the spaghetti is cooked al dente, drain it and pour it into a serving dish, add the cream mix, the melted butter and the grated ricotta, stir and serve.

• Spaghetti with walnuts •

400 g of spaghetti, salt, 12 walnuts, 1 glass of single cream,
30 g of butter, a few sprigs of parsley, pepper.

Remove the walnuts from their shells and remove the skin, place in a blender; add about half of the cream and blend for a few minutes until smooth. Melt the butter in a small saucepan, add the walnut mix, the remaining cream and the washed and chopped parsley.

Season with salt and a little pepper, place on a moderate heat and allow to thicken, stirring often with a wooden spoon. In the meantime cook the spaghetti in plenty of salted boiling water, then drain and pour into a serving dish, add the walnut sauce, mix thoroughly and serve immediately.

• Spaghetti with truffle •

400 g of spaghetti, salt, 1 packet of saffron,
extra virgin olive oil, 100 g of bacon rashers, 1 sprig of parsley,
1 small black truffle (or truffle paste).

This recipe, with truffle, is very easy to prepare: if you have no fresh truffle then you can use a good quality truffle paste, which will also allow you to prepare the sauce in less time. Put a pan of water on to heat, when it is boiling salt the water and add the saffron and the spaghetti.

While the pasta is cooking, heat 1 dessert spoon of oil in

quite a wide frying pan, add the rashers of bacon, cut into strips, and allow to cook until crispy. Add the drained pasta, plenty of chopped parsley and the truffle, which you have trimmed, washed and sliced thinly, or the truffle paste if you are using it. Sauté for a couple of minutes and then serve, adding a drop of olive oil if necessary.

• Spaghetti with pine nuts •

400 g of spaghetti, salt, a few sprigs of parsley,
50 g of pine nuts, 3 dessert spoons of extra virgin olive oil,
1/2 a medium onion, pepper, 2 dessert spoons of vodka,
5 dessert spoons of grated parmesan cheese.

Put a pan of water on to heat, when it is boiling add some salt and the spaghetti, leave to cook. In the meantime prepare the sauce: trim the parsley, wash and dry it and chop it finely, roughly chop the pine nuts. Pour the oil into a saucepan, add the peeled and thinly sliced onion and sauté for a few minutes, then add the parsley, the pine nuts, salt and pepper. Leave to cook on a moderate heat for 5 minutes, sprinkle with the vodka and, as soon as it has evaporated remove from the heat.

When the pasta is cooked al dente, drain it and pour it into a serving dish, add the sauce and sprinkle with the grated parmesan cheese. Serve.

• Friday's spaghetti •

400 g of spaghetti, salt, 1 sprig of parsley, 4 salted anchovies,
4 dessert spoons of extra virgin olive oil, 2 cloves of garlic,
30 g of butter, 2 dessert spoons of grated parmesan cheese,
2 dessert spoons of mature ricotta cheese, grated.

At one time Friday was a day of abstinence on which no meat was eaten, sometimes people even fasted, in compliance with precepts of the church, which were given much more importance in daily life compared to today. Certainly nowadays these customs are no longer so closely followed, except on particular occasions. This recipe for Friday's spaghetti despite not containing a meat sauce, is still very tasty, nor can it be considered a dish which imposes certain sacrifices. It is easy to make and takes very little time and the combination of anchovies and mature ricotta cheese makes it full of flavour.

Put some water on to heat and when it boils add some salt and the pasta. In the meantime trim, wash, dry and finely chop the parsley, then rinse the anchovies and remove the bones, chop them into small pieces. Heat the oil in a saucepan, squash the cloves of garlic slightly, without removing the outer skin and fry them in the oil until golden brown, then discard, add the parsley and the anchovies to the oil. Allow the anchovies to melt then remove from the heat.

When the pasta is cooked, drain it, and pour it into a serving dish, add the butter, the anchovy oil and the grated cheeses. Stir well.

CURRY

This mix of oriental spices, is ready to use and is quite well known also in the west. It is used to flavour rice, soups, vegetables, pulses and it can enrich numerous sauces.

The mix, called masala in traditional Indian cuisine, which uses it in great quantities, can be of varying strengths and its typical composition is usually based on turmeric, coriander, white pepper, cinnamon, cardamom, cumin, chilli, ginger and asafoetida. The mixes that are usually found in the shops are often quite lacking in flavour and the best thing to do is buy the mix from a specialist grocer's or from one of the shops that sell specialist products from all around the world, these shops can be found in most large cities.

• Spaghetti with anchovies •

400 g of spaghetti, salt, 5 salted anchovies,
1/2 a glass of extra virgin olive oil, 2 cloves of garlic, pepper,
2 dessert spoons of grated parmesan cheese,
2 dessert spoons of mature ricotta cheese, grated.

A few essential ingredients make this a very simple dish to prepare. Although that certainly doesn't mean that it is lacking in flavour. Rinse the anchovies under cold running water, discard the bones and chop the anchovies into small pieces. Heat the oil in a saucepan, squash the cloves of garlic slightly and fry them in the oil until golden brown, then discard, add the anchovies to the oil.

Allow them to melt, squashing them with a wooden spoon, season with a little freshly ground pepper and remove from the heat. In the meantime cook the pasta in plenty of salted, boiling water and, when it is cooked drain it well and add the anchovy sauce and the grated cheeses. Mix thoroughly and serve without delay.

• Sweet spaghetti •

400 g of spaghetti, salt, 100 g of sultanas, 100 g of pine nuts, extra virgin olive oil, 1 teaspoon of curry powder, a little milk.

Wash the sultanas and leave them to soak in a little water for 1/4 of an hour: then prepare the sauce and at the same time cook the spaghetti in plenty of salted, boiling water. Heat a little milk in a saucepan and mix in the drained sultanas, the pine nuts, the curry and a pinch of salt, then drain the spaghetti and add the sauce to it.

Pour the spaghetti into a greased, ovenproof dish and place in a hot oven for 8-10 minutes, until a thin crust forms. Meanwhile serve some raw, seasonal vegetables as a tasty appetiser.

• Spaghetti
with gorgonzola cheese •

*400 g of spaghetti, salt, 100 g of gorgonzola cheese,
2 dl of milk, 200 g of fresh ricotta cheese, 50 g of butter,
1 celery stalk, 1/2 an onion, pepper.*

Not everybody likes gorgonzola cheese, due to its quite sharp taste. Make sure that your guests like it and then begin: with very little effort you will be able to offer a really delicious dish. Put the gorgonzola, the ricotta and the milk in a blender and blend until smooth, on medium speed. Put this creamy mixture into a bowl and mix thoroughly with the washed and finely chopped onion and celery, a little salt and pepper and a little milk.

In the meantime cook the pasta in plenty of salted, boiling water and, when it is cooked drain and pour into a serving dish, add the butter, which has been allowed to soften at room temperature, and the gorgonzola mixture which has been diluted, at the last minute with a couple of spoonfuls of the pasta water.

• Spaghetti with dry bread •

400 g of spaghetti, salt, 8 dessert spoons of extra virgin olive oil, 100 g of dry bread, pepper, a few sprigs of parsley.

Spaghetti with dry bread is, without doubt, a very plain and simple dish, but nonetheless very tasty. It is a very old

dish and typical of some areas of Italy, where it is still very popular. Break the bread up into large crumbs put them in a frying pan with the oil and allow to fry until golden brown, careful not to let them burn, season with salt and pepper.

Cook the spaghetti in plenty of salted, boiling water and, when it is cooked drain and pour into a serving dish, add the bread and the washed and finely chopped parsley. To further enrich the flavour you can add a clove of garlic to the oil as you are heating it and then discard before adding the dry bread.

• Spaghetti with sour cream •

400 g of spaghetti, salt, 60 g of butter, 2 dl of sour cream, 100 g of parmesan cheese, paprika powder.

Put some water on to heat and when it is boiling add some salt and cook the spaghetti. In the meantime gently melt the butter in a large saucepan.

When the pasta is cooked al dente, drain it and pour it into the saucepan with the butter, stir well and add the sour cream, the paprika and a little grated parmesan cheese. Stir for a little longer and then serve immediately, serve the rest of the parmesan cheese separately.

If you think it needs a little more flavour you can add some grated nutmeg.

• Spaghetti with capers •

400 g of spaghetti, salt, 100 g of salted capers,
1/2 a glass of extra virgin olive oil, oregano,
3 dessert spoons of grated parmesan cheese,
pepper or red chilli powder.

Capers are one of those gifts from heaven that, in their simplicity, allow you to create tasty and pleasing dishes in any season, but particularly in summer: a spoonful of these tiny buds is able to give vitality to the simplest of lunches. For this recipe you should first rinse the capers under running water to get rid of the salt, then you must chop them roughly and put them in a bowl.

Add some olive oil and a good pinch of oregano, the grated cheese, a pinch of salt and a pinch of pepper or red chilli pepper, depending on personal taste.

Now put the water on to heat and when it is boiling add the salt and then cook the spaghetti. Finally, drain the spaghetti and pour it into the serving dish with the capers, stir thoroughly and serve hot, but if you prefer, also cold.

• Spaghetti with rocket •

400 g of spaghetti, salt, 150 g of fresh rocket leaves,
1 small onion, 200 g of firm, ripe tomatoes,
1/2 a glass of extra virgin olive oil, red chilli powder,
4 dessert spoons of grated pecorino cheese.

Rocket grows spontaneously throughout the year so it is not difficult to pick some whilst out on a walk, as long as you are sure that there is no risk of pollution.

The wild varieties usually have much more flavour than the cultivated varieties, but if you have no other possibility it is obvious that you will have to use the latter, which will still be able to enrich your spaghetti. Firstly trim, wash and dry the rocket, using a salad spinner if possible. Then peel the onion, and chop it finely, put in a serving dish with the washed and diced raw tomatoes, the oil, some salt and a pinch of red chilli powder.

Then tear the rocket into pieces and add to the other ingredients, mix thoroughly. Put some water on to heat and when it boils, add some salt and cook the spaghetti, when cooked drain and pour into the serving dish, stir well and serve after a couple of minutes.

• Rustic spaghetti •

400 g of spaghetti, salt, about ten sage leaves, 2 cloves of garlic, 1 bunch of parsley, 4 basil leaves, red chilli powder, about ten dessert spoons of extra virgin olive oil.

It doesn't take a lot to prepare this simple and appetising dish: just a few ingredients that are readily available and a touch of flavour added by the red chilli. It is very quick to prepare while the spaghetti is cooking, and goes especially well with wholewheat pasta.

Pour the oil into a frying pan and fry the sage leaves and

the crushed garlic cloves, being careful not to let them burn: stir often with a wooden spoon and keep the heat quite low. Just before removing from the heat add the finely chopped basil and the washed and finely chopped parsley. Meanwhile put some water on to heat and when it boils add some salt and the spaghetti.

When the spaghetti is al dente, drain and pour into the serving dish, add the sauce and maybe a drop of olive oil. Stir and serve immediately.

• Spaghetti with ricotta cheese •

400 g of spaghetti, salt,
1/2 a glass of extra virgin olive oil, 1 teaspoon of paprika,
150 g of fresh ricotta cheese, salt.

Using good fresh ricotta, made from goat's or sheep's milk will give the sauce a very particular flavour, but even with fresh cow's milk ricotta, especially home made, you should have nothing to complain about.

While the pasta is cooking in plenty of salted, boiling water, prepare a simple sauce by pouring the oil into a dish, add the paprika, the crumbled up ricotta and some salt. Mix thoroughly in order to blend the flavours, and add, if you think it necessary, a few spoonfuls of the cooking water of the pasta.

When the spaghetti is cooked, drain and pour into the serving dish and add the ricotta and paprika sauce, stir very thoroughly and serve immediately.

• Recipes
with vegetables •

Spaghetti served with vegetables and enriched with appetising aromatic herbs is perhaps the most typical dish of Mediterranean cuisine and there are plenty of recipes to choose from. Certainly it is rare to forego tomato, because the tradition of serving spaghetti with this sauce is deep-rooted and, much appreciated, but with almost all vegetables it is possible to make very tasty sauces, and they are, almost always, quite easy to prepare. So, depending on the season, without having to rely on the so-called "early vegetables", we can make use of radicchio or cauliflower, artichokes or aubergines, peas or peppers, asparagus or fennel. A different dish every day, to satisfy everyone's tastes, and offer plenty of variety.

• Spaghetti with tomato •

400 g of spaghetti, salt, 800 g of ripe tomatoes, 5 dessert spoons of extra virgin olive oil, red chilli powder, a few basil leaves, grated parmesan or pecorino cheese.

There are many variations on how to make a spaghetti sauce with tomato, the following recipe is just one of them. First put a pan of water on to heat, when it boils plunge the tomatoes into the water for a moment, so that the skin begins to split and they are easier to peel.

After having peeled them, remove the seeds and put them through a vegetable mill.

If they are very watery cut them in half after you have peeled them and leave them on a sloping surface for a 1/4 of an hour before putting through the vegetable mill.

In either case, after having done this put the tomatoes in a saucepan on a moderate heat, add the oil and, after about a 1/2 of an hour add some salt and some red chilli powder to taste. Continue to cook for as long as you think necessary (usually less than an hour is enough).

At the end of cooking add the finally chopped basil leaves.

Next put a pan of water on to heat for the pasta and when it boils add some salt and cook the spaghetti. When it is al dente drain the spaghetti and transfer it to a serving dish, add the tomato sauce and stir well.

Serve immediately with some grated parmesan cheese.

• Spicy spaghetti •

*400 g of spaghetti, salt, 400 g of ripe tomatoes,
1 medium size onion, 1 clove of garlic, 1/2 a glass of extra
virgin olive oil, red chilli pepper in powder or pieces,
2 dessert spoons of grated parmesan cheese,
2 dessert spoons of grated pecorino cheese.*

The concept of "spicy" obviously depends on personal tastes and so, in the case of the sauce suggested in this recipe, the amount of red chilli pepper in powder, or in small pieces, to use is left to your discretion. In any case, before doing anything else plunge the tomatoes in boiling water to remove the skins, remove the seeds and finely chop them.

Then finely chop the onion together with the garlic. Next heat the oil in a small saucepan, add the onion and garlic and allow to sauté for a few minutes on a moderate heat. Then add the tomatoes and the chilli powder or pieces of chilli pepper, season with salt, cover and simmer for about ten minutes.

In the meantime put a pan of water on to heat and, when it boils, add some salt and cook the spaghetti. When cooked drain the spaghetti, pour it into a serving dish and add the spicy sauce. Just before serving sprinkle with the mixed grated cheeses.

• Sicilian spaghetti •

400 g of spaghetti, salt, 1/2 a glass of extra virgin olive oil,
2 cloves of garlic, 500 g of ripe San Marzano tomatoes,
1 medium size aubergine, red chilli powder, 1 yellow pepper,
4 salted anchovies, 5 black olives, 1 dessert spoon
of salted capers, a few basil leaves.

This Sicilian spaghetti is characterised by a typically Mediterranean sauce, rich in flavour and colour. First heat the oil, add the garlic and when it is golden brown, discard. Add the peeled, de-seeded, chopped tomatoes and the peeled, diced aubergine. Season with salt and red chilli powder and leave to cook on a moderate heat for about half an hour, stirring from time to time with a wooden spoon. Meanwhile grill the pepper, discarding the skin, cut into strips; then rinse the anchovies under cold running water and carefully remove all the bones.

Just before removing the tomato sauce from the heat, add the peppers, the anchovies, the pitted olives, the rinsed capers and the chopped basil. Next put the water on to heat for the pasta, when it boils add the salt and cook the spaghetti until al dente.

When it is cooked, drain the spaghetti and pour into a serving dish, add the sauce and serve.

• Neapolitan spaghetti •

400 g of spaghetti, salt, 3 dessert spoons of extra virgin olive oil, 80 g of butter, 1 medium size onion, 800 g of ripe tomatoes, a few basil leaves (at least 5 or 6), a pinch of red chilli powder, 4 dessert spoons of grated caciocavallo cheese.

The imagination of the Neapolitans has enriched our dining tables with countless pasta sauces. Without fail, tomato can be found in all of them and in this recipe there is a special touch provided by the magnificent union between caciocavallo cheese, basil and onion. First plunge the tomatoes in boiling water, peel them, remove the seeds and chop them. Heat the oil and half of the butter in a saucepan, add the onion, sliced quite thickly and sauté. Then discard the onion and add the chopped tomato to the oil, add the basil leaves, season with salt and a little chilli powder and cook for about ten minutes on quite a high

BASIL

A typically Mediterranean herb, widely used and with an unmistakable aroma, it is used in many different dishes, but also boasts many beneficial properties. Phytotherapy acknowledges its capacity to benefit the nervous system, to calm coughs, to aid digestion and to have positive diuretic affects. The tea made from basil is used externally for rinsing, gargling, beauty washes, the cleansing and health of the skin or for the preparation of toning baths.

heat, so that the sauce thickens. In the meantime cook the spaghetti in plenty of salted, boiling water, then drain and pour into a warmed serving dish. Add the remaining butter and the tomato sauce, sprinkle with the grated cheese, stir thoroughly and serve.

• Aromatic spaghetti •

400 g of spaghetti, salt, 2 cloves of garlic, 1 bunch of parsley, 1 small piece of red chilli pepper, 400 g of ripe tomatoes, 4 dessert spoons of extra virgin olive oil, 1 dessert spoon of finely chopped rosemary, 1 dessert spoon of wholewheat flour, 1 dessert spoon of butter (about 20 g), 4 dessert spoons of grated parmesan cheese.

Peel the tomatoes by plunging them into boiling water, remove the seeds and roughly chop, then finely chop the garlic together with the trimmed, washed and dried parsley and the piece of chilli pepper. Heat the oil in a saucepan and add the tomatoes, cook them on a high heat for a moment then add the garlic mixture prepared previously and the rosemary, season with salt and allow to simmer for about five minutes, stirring from time to time with a wooden spoon. Just before removing from the heat add the flour which has been blended with the butter. In the meantime cook the spaghetti in plenty of salted, boiling water and when it is al dente, drain and transfer to a suitable serving dish, add the sauce and stir well. Before serving sprinkle with the grated parmesan cheese.

• Vegetable spaghetti carbonara •

*400 g of pasta, salt, 6 medium size courgettes, 1 onion,
1/2 a yellow pepper, 1 cabbage leaf, 7 dessert spoons of extra
virgin olive oil, 2 eggs, nutmeg, grated parmesan cheese.*

To begin with, prepare the vegetables: trim, wash and dry
them, then slice the onion and the cabbage and cut the
courgettes and pepper into small pieces. Heat 5 dessert
spoons of oil in a frying pan and sauté the vegetables,
starting with the onion, then adding the pepper, then the
cabbage and lastly the courgettes.
Season with a little salt, cover and simmer for about a 1/4
of an hour. In the meantime put the water on for the pasta, when it boils add the salt and cook the spaghetti.
When it is cooked drain the spaghetti and pour it into the
frying pan with the vegetables, add the remaining oil and
the two eggs, beaten with a little nutmeg, leave to cook
for another couple of minutes to allow the flavours to
mingle, stir with a wooden spoon, then serve, offering
grated parmesan cheese.

• Spaghetti with courgettes •

*400 g of spaghetti, salt, 8 medium size courgettes,
6 dessert spoons of extra virgin olive oil, 2 cloves of garlic,
8 basil leaves, 2 eggs, pepper.*

In this recipe the courgettes are the main attraction but
are enriched by the addition of eggs, which make this dish

a little more filling and tasty. Trim the courgettes, wash and dry them and slice them thinly into rounds. Heat the oil in a frying pan and sauté the crushed garlic. When the garlic is golden brown discard it and add the courgettes to the oil, turn down the heat, cover and cook on a low heat.When the courgettes are almost cooked add the chopped basil and season to taste with a little pepper. Put the water on to heat for the pasta and, when it boils add the salt and cook the spaghetti, draining when al dente. Beat the egg in the serving dish and add the spaghetti and the courgettes, mix thoroughly. Wait a couple of minutes to give the egg time to set a little and then serve. If you prefer you can offer some grated parmesan cheese with this dish.

• Spaghetti from Bari •

*400 g of spaghetti, salt, 1 kg of turnip tops,
250 g of ripe tomatoes, 1 bunch of basil, 2 dessert spoons
of extra virgin olive oil, 2 dessert spoons of lard,
2 cloves of garlic.*

This is a typical rustic dish, fresh and full of flavour, and easy to prepare. Firstly see to the turnip tops, trim and wash them, you can put aside the very top part to use in another dish or for soup. Put a pan of water on to heat and when it boils plunge the tomatoes in it so as to be able to peel them easily. Then remove the seeds and put the tomatoes through a vegetable mill. Put a large pan of water on to heat and when it boils add the salt and put the spaghetti and the turnip tops in together to cook. In the meantime heat the oil, in a frying pan, with the crushed garlic and the lard: sauté without burning and after having drained the al dente pasta add this oil to it, add the tomato sauce and the chopped basil, stir thoroughly and serve with a good, cold, white wine.

• Tasty spaghetti •

400 g of spaghetti, salt, 7 dessert spoons of extra virgin olive oil, 1 piece of chilli pepper, 1 medium size onion, 2 cloves of garlic, 6 fresh mint leaves, a few celery leaves, 800 g of firm, ripe plum tomatoes, 1 bunch of parsley, grated pecorino cheese.

The pungent aroma of the fresh mint gives this dish a very special flavour. Try to always keep a plant on the balcony of your home: it doesn't need any special attention and it can be used in many different dishes. Heat the oil in a frying pan, add the chilli pepper and when it has flavoured the oil add the finely sliced onion, sauté on a moderate heat then add the finely sliced garlic. Next add the finely chopped mint leaves, the celery leaves, peel and de-seed the tomatoes and cut them into strips, add to the other ingredients in the frying pan. Season to taste with a little salt, cover and allow to cook on a low heat, stirring with a wooden spoon from time to time. Allow the sauce to thicken, but if it seems to be drying up too quickly you could add a little warm water. When it is almost cooked add the chopped parsley then remove from the heat. Put a pan of water on to heat and when it boils add some salt and cook the pasta, then drain and pour into a serving dish, add the sauce and serve, offering some grated pecorino cheese. If you prefer you can remove the garlic from the frying pan before adding the tomatoes.

• Spaghetti primavera •

400 g of spaghetti, salt, 1 medium size onion, 4 carrots,
1 head of celery, 2 courgettes, 100 g of shelled peas,
6 dessert spoons of extra virgin olive oil, 1 bunch of parsley,
grated parmesan cheese.

Peel the onion, slice it and sauté it in a frying pan with the oil, stirring to avoid burning. Wash the carrots and courgettes and slice them into rounds, wash and chop up the celery, add these and the peas to the oil. Allow the vegetables to simmer, covered, over a moderate heat and when almost ready add a little salt. Then add the trimmed, washed and chopped parsley. Put a pan of water on to heat for the pasta, when it boils add the salt and cook the spaghetti. When al dente, drain and pour into a serving dish, add the vegetable sauce, serve offering grated parmesan cheese. If you have some "gomasio", a seasoning much used by health food lovers, made with toasted sesame seeds and unrefined sea salt which are crushed with a pestle and mortar, now is the time to use it. Sprinkle a

MINT

The mint family is one of the most complex in the vegetable kingdom, as there are many different varieties, there are over a hundred, distributed across all the temperate regions of the globe and they are, mostly, intermediate hybrids. They are plants that spread very quickly, and are believed to have various important properties, which means that they are used in phytotherapy and in the composition of various cosmetic products. The principal ingredient of drugs is the essential oil; there are also various acids present, antibiotic substances, enzymes and vitamin C. The use of fresh leaves is indicated in various dishes, to which they can add a very particular and stimulating aroma.

couple of teaspoons over the spaghetti, instead of the grated cheese, just before serving.

• Spaghetti with parsley and basil •

400 g of spaghetti, salt, 400 g of firm, ripe tomatoes,
6 dessert spoons of extra virgin olive oil, 1 bunch of parsley,
a few basil leaves, 2 cloves of garlic, red chilli pepper
or chilli powder, 1 small piece of root ginger,
150 g of fresh mozzarella cheese.

This is another decidedly summery recipe: this dish is characterised by the abundant use of parsley and basil, but the use of grated ginger gives an unusual touch. Plunge the tomatoes in boiling water so that they are easier to peel. Then remove the seeds and chop them, put them in a saucepan with the oil and cook on a moderate heat until they thicken. In the meantime prepare a mix with plenty of washed and dried parsley, plenty of basil leaves, the cloves of garlic and a small piece of chilli pepper all finely chopped, add the grated ginger. Put a pan of water on to heat for the pasta, when it boils add the salt and cook the spaghetti until al dente, drain. Add the parsley mixture to the tomato sauce, season with salt and add to the spaghetti along with the cubed mozzarella, stir thoroughly so that the heat of the spaghetti can melt the cheese and serve, sprinkling with a little more chopped parsley.

• Spaghetti with radicchio •

400 g of spaghetti, salt, 400 g of red radicchio, 1/2 an onion, 6 dessert spoons of extra virgin olive oil, pepper, nutmeg, 1/2 a glass of single cream, 150 g of fontina cheese.

Spaghetti with radicchio is a dish which is made particularly in winter, when radicchio is fresh and full of flavour. The typical bitter flavour of the radicchio is softened by the presence of the cream and the fontina cheese. Remove most of the roots from the radicchio then wash it and cut into strips, a couple of millimetres wide. Peel and finely chop the onion then sauté it with the oil in a frying pan, add the radicchio, cover, and allow to stew, place a flame

diffuser under the pan if possible. When the radicchio is cooked season with salt, pepper and a pinch of nutmeg, then add the cream and leave to cook for another 4 or 5 minutes, stirring with a wooden spoon. Put a pan of water on for the pasta and when it boils add some salt and cook the spaghetti al dente. Drain the spaghetti and pour it into the frying pan with the radicchio, add the cubes of fontina cheese and stir thoroughly, pour the spaghetti into a serving dish and serve.

• Spaghetti with onions •

400 g of spaghetti, salt, 5 firm, ripe tomatoes, 3 onions, oregano, 6 dessert spoons of extra virgin olive oil.

The preparation of the sauce for this recipe, for which very thin spaghetti is ideal, does not present any particular difficulties; however it requires quite a long soaking time so you must programme well in advance. Wash, dry and chop the tomatoes, put them in a serving dish along with their juice, add the peeled and finely sliced onions, a generous pinch of oregano and the oil, then leave to soak, for at least 8 hours, in a cool place.

When you are ready to eat put the water on to heat for the pasta, when it boils add the salt and cook the spaghetti, drain carefully when cooked then pour into the serving dish with the tomatoes and onions, mix thoroughly to combine all the flavours then serve, adding a drop of olive oil if preferred.

GINGER

The knobbly, brown rhizome of the Zingiber officinale widely used fresh or powdered in traditional Indian or Chinese cookery, can also be found in certain dishes typical of our country. Its particular, tempting aroma gives them an unmistakable flavour.

It is also sold in powdered form, but the best way to use it is to buy it fresh and grate it as needed. In the east it is used as a cure for colic and dyspepsia, and also for sore throats and hoarseness; it is also commonly considered to be a good digestive and is often used in the preparation of apéritifs.

• Spaghetti with mushrooms •

400 g of spaghetti, salt, 300 g of wild mushrooms, 3 cloves of garlic, 8 dessert spoons of extra virgin olive oil, red chilli powder, 100 ml of single cream, 1 bunch of parsley.

The best way to make a very good sauce is to use a good variety of wild mushrooms, but if this just isn't possible, obviously you can use cultivated mushrooms. Clean the mushrooms, removing any inedible parts or soil, wash them very quickly under cold, running water, avoid wetting them too much. Dry them thoroughly and slice them, put them straight into a frying pan with the oil and the crushed garlic.

Cook them on a high heat for about five minutes and then

lower the heat and simmer, adding salt and chilli powder, and the cream just before removing from the heat. Put a pan of water on for the pasta, when the water boils cook the spaghetti until al dente.

Drain the spaghetti and pour it into a serving dish, mix in the mushrooms, sprinkle with the chopped parsley and finally add a drop of olive oil if you wish.

• Spaghetti
with mushrooms and peppers •

*400 g of spaghetti, salt, 1 small onion, 1 clove of garlic,
8 dessert spoons of extra virgin olive oil, 30 g of dried
mushrooms, 1 medium size green pepper,
200 g of tinned tomatoes, 6 basil leaves, pepper.*

Peel and finely chop the onion, then peel and finely chop the garlic. Put the oil in a saucepan, heat it and add the onion and garlic, sauté, stirring with a wooden spoon then add the mushrooms, which you have previously soaked and then drained. Wash, de-seed and roughly chop the pepper and add it to the mushrooms, then add a little warm water and 3 finely chopped basil leaves.

Allow to simmer over a moderate heat for about twenty minutes, stirring from time to time, add the remaining whole basil leaves and remove the pan from the heat. Now put a pan of water on to heat for the spaghetti.

When the water begins to boil add the salt and cook the spaghetti until al dente. Then drain and pour into a serv-

ing dish, add the sauce and season with pepper to taste. Serve with a bottle of cold white wine, for example Pinot grigio.

• Spaghetti
with mushrooms and tomato •

400 g of spaghetti, salt, 200 g of mushrooms,
8 dessert spoons of extra virgin olive oil, 300 g of firm,
ripe tomatoes, pepper, 1 bunch of parsley,
4 dessert spoons of grated parmesan cheese.

If it is possible to use wild mushrooms, all the better; but if you have no other choice than to use cultivated mushrooms, don't worry. The spaghetti will be tasty and appetising all the same. Begin by cleaning the mushrooms: carefully remove any soil and inedible parts, wash them quickly under cold running water, dry and slice them. Put them in a frying pan with the oil and tomatoes, which have been peeled and put through a vegetable mill.

After a few minutes of cooking on a high heat, cover and allow to simmer for about half an hour, season with salt and pepper just before removing from the heat. Now put a pan of water on to heat for the spaghetti. When the water begins to boil add the salt and cook the spaghetti until al dente. Then drain and pour into a serving dish, add the tomato sauce and the washed, chopped parsley.

Serve immediately, offering grated parmesan cheese and a good, cold, dry white wine.

• Spaghetti with peppers •

400 g of spaghetti, salt, 1 green pepper, 1 large yellow pepper, 8 dessert spoons of extra virgin olive oil, 1 dessert spoon of curry powder, 5 fresh basil leaves, 2 cloves of garlic.

First wash the peppers, dry them, remove the stalks and the seeds and cut them into strips. Then fry them in a frying pan with the oil for a few minutes, then lower the flame, add the curry powder and allow to soften, covered for about twenty minutes, stir every so often with a wooden spoon and season with salt just before removing from the heat. Now cook the pasta: put a pan of water on to heat, when it boils add the spaghetti.

When it is cooked drain and pour into the frying pan with the peppers, add the roughly chopped basil leaves, the finely sliced garlic and a drop of olive oil. Lastly, stir very thoroughly and leave on the heat for just a couple of minutes before serving.

• Spaghetti with pumpkin •

*400 g of spaghetti, salt, 600 g of pumpkin, 1 small onion,
200 g of firm, ripe tomatoes, 40 g of single cream,
4 dessert spoons of grated pecorino cheese, pepper.*

Remove the thick, hard skin from the pumpkin, discard the seeds and cut the flesh into quite small cubes. Plunge the tomatoes in boiling water, so that they can be peeled without difficulty, cut them into pieces and remove the seeds. Cook the pumpkin in a frying pan with the oil, the chopped onion and the chopped tomatoes: after a few minutes on a high heat lower, cover and simmer for about twenty minutes, add a little salt just before removing from the heat. Put a pan of water on for the pasta, when the water boils add the salt and cook the spaghetti until al dente.
Drain the spaghetti and pour into a serving dish, add the tomato and pumpkin sauce, the cream, the grated pecorino cheese and a little freshly ground black pepper, stir thoroughly and serve.

• Spaghetti with peas •

*400 g of spaghetti, salt, 8 dessert spoons of extra virgin olive
oil, 500 g of freshly shelled peas, 2 medium size onions,
1 carrot, 1/4 dl of single cream, 1 bunch of parsley.*

The use of fresh peas guarantees more flavour and substance to this spaghetti sauce: the unhealthy habit of resorting to the use of tinned or packet foods, unless occasional, is not very good from a nutritional point of view. This is particularly true as regards peas, a vegetable which is very often served after having been preserved in a tin or frozen. First put the peas in a frying pan with the oil, add the carrot, which has been washed, dried and diced, and the finely chopped onion.

Fry the vegetables on a high heat for a few minutes then add a little warm water and allow to cook, covered, on a moderate heat for about half an hour. When the vegetables are cooked add the cream and leave on the heat for a moment. Put a pan of water on to heat for the spaghetti, when the water boils add the pasta.

When it is cooked drain it and pour it into a serving dish, add the vegetables and the chopped parsley.

• Spaghetti with asparagus •

400 g of spaghetti, salt, 1 kg of asparagus,
extra virgin olive oil, 250 g of fresh ricotta, pepper,
2 eggs, nutmeg, grated parmesan cheese.

Trim the asparagus, removing the woody part and cook them in salted, boiling water for about a 1/4 of an hour, drain and leave to drip, then cut them into small pieces, discarding any parts that are still hard.

Heat the oil in a large frying pan, add the pieces of asparagus and sauté, meanwhile crumble the ricotta into a bowl and blend it with a little warm water and some salt and pepper until creamy. Put a pan of water on to heat for the spaghetti: when the water boils add the salt and cook the spaghetti until al dente, meanwhile grease a baking tin with oil. When the pasta is cooked drain it and season it with oil and grated parmesan cheese, make a layer, with some of the spaghetti in the baking tin, top with some of the asparagus and half of the ricotta.

Then continue with a layer of spaghetti, the remaining asparagus and the ricotta, finish with another layer of spaghetti. Beat the eggs with a little salt and pepper, a pinch of nutmeg and a couple of dessert spoons of grated parmesan cheese, pour over the top of the spaghetti. Put the baking tin in a pre-heated oven and bake for about half an hour.

• Spaghetti with artichokes •

400 g of spaghetti, salt, 2 eggs, 4 artichokes, 1 lemon,
2 dessert spoons of extra virgin olive oil, 30 g of butter,
1/2 a glass of dry white wine, pepper.

Boil the eggs until hard, about 10 minutes from when the water starts to boil. Then drain them, cool under cold running water and shell. Trim the artichokes, discarding the harder leaves, slice the others thinly and put them to soak in water and lemon juice.

Heat the oil and half of the butter in a saucepan, add the well drained artichokes and allow to cook for a few minutes, then sprinkle with the white wine, season with salt and pepper and simmer on a low heat for about half an hour. Cut the boiled eggs in half, put the yolks in a dish and dice the whites, put in a serving dish. Add the remaining butter to the egg yolks and mix well with a fork, when the artichokes are almost cooked add the egg yolk mixture.

Put a pan of water on to heat for the spaghetti: when it boils add the salt and cook the pasta until al dente, drain and pour into the serving dish with the egg whites, add the artichokes and stir thoroughly before serving.

• Spaghetti with fennel •

400 g of spaghetti, salt, 1 fennel of about 200 g, 1 onion,
6 dessert spoons of extra virgin olive oil, 50 g of sultanas,
50 g of pine nuts, grated parmesan cheese (optional).

Other than being full of flavour fennel also boasts various other virtues: it stimulates secretion of saliva, stimulates appetite and is a good diuretic, it aids lactation and it seems that it can cure diarrhoea, vomiting and hiccoughs, as well as solving menstrual problems and decreasing azotaemia. But for now we shall content ourselves with using it to flavour a good spaghetti dish.

Clean the fennel and steam, or if you prefer, cook in salted water. Drain carefully and keep the cooking water. Peel and finely chop the onion, then put it into a frying pan with the oil and cook on a moderate heat, stir with a wooden spoon to avoid burning. When it is soft add the finely chopped fennel, the pine nuts and the sultanas which have been left to soak in a little water and then drained. Season with salt and pepper and leave to cook for a few minutes, to allow the flavours to mingle. Meanwhile cook the spaghetti in the cooking water from the fennel, with the addition of more salted water. When the pasta is cooked drain it and pour into a serving dish, add the hot sauce and serve, offering grated parmesan cheese.

• Spaghetti with aubergines •

400 g of spaghetti, salt, 3 long aubergines, 2 cloves of garlic, extra virgin olive oil, 1 bunch of parsley.

Spaghetti with aubergines, a typical summer dish, certainly isn't difficult to prepare: however, the aubergines must be fried, so this takes a little time. Trim, wash and dry the aubergines and then cut them into wide, not too thin, slices, place the slices on a sloping surface and sprinkle them with sea salt, so that the water in them drains away and they lose their slightly bitter taste.

After a couple of hours drain them well and fry them in a frying pan with plenty of oil and the crushed garlic. After frying place them on absorbent kitchen paper, in order to remove the excess oil.

Put a pan of water on to heat for the pasta, when it boils add the salt and cook the spaghetti.

When it is al dente drain the spaghetti and pour it into a serving dish, add the aubergines and stir well, sprinkling with chopped parsley. Serve immediately.

• Spaghetti with cauliflower •

400 g of spaghetti, salt, 1 medium size cauliflower, 3 dessert spoons of olive paste, a pinch of marjoram, nutmeg, extra virgin olive oil, grated parmesan cheese (optional).

The cauliflower is a vegetable which is widely used in cooking, both raw and cooked, as well as recommended in phytotherapy in cases of asthenia, weakness, influenza and colds. It is an excellent accompaniment to spaghetti.

Remove the leaves and the tough parts from the cauliflower, wash it and divide into florets, cook for about ten minutes in plenty of salted, boiling water.

Add the spaghetti to the same pan and cook until al dente. Drain the cauliflower and spaghetti and pour into a serving dish, add the olive paste, the marjoram, the nutmeg and oil to taste. Stir thoroughly and serve, offering grated parmesan cheese if you wish.

• Spaghetti with beans •

280 g of spaghetti, 120 g of dried beans (butter beans if possible), 2 bay leaves, 1 sprig of rosemary, about 10 chives, 1 dessert spoon of chopped tarragon, pepper, extra virgin olive oil, grated parmesan cheese (optional).

Begin by washing the beans and leaving them to soak in cold water, with the bay leaves, for at least 12 hours, then remove them from the water, discard the bay leaves, and put the beans in a saucepan with fresh water and the rosemary, place on a moderate heat and when cooked drain, keeping the cooking water ready for the spaghetti, put the beans through a sieve, reducing them to a puree, if necessary add a little of the cooking water until creamy, add a little oil, the chopped chives and the tarragon, season with salt and pepper and mix thoroughly, now, without delay, cook the spaghetti. Put a pan on to heat with the cooking water from the beans, plus some more water, when it boils add the salt and cook the pasta until al dente. Then drain and pour into a serving dish, add the creamed beans and, if necessary a drop of olive oil. Serve immediately, offering grated parmesan cheese if desired.

• Spaghetti albese •

400 g of spaghetti, salt, 1 medium size white truffle, 70 g of butter, grated parmesan cheese, pepper, nutmeg, 1/2 a cup of meat stock, 3 dessert spoons of roast gravy.

LEGUMES

It is necessary to follow a few simple rules when preparing and eating dried beans, and, indeed, all dried legumes, in order to make them more digestible and limit their harmfulness. In fact, although they are very nutritious, legumes contain some toxic elements which can have harmful effects if consumed in great quantities. The fibrous skin which surrounds them can cause troublesome, although not harmful, intestinal gas. These problems can be solved by adequate soaking, the right cooking, adequate chewing and the eventual use of "mashers" to remove the skins. The soaking water should be thrown away and substituted with fresh water for cooking: in fact soaking is not only to soften the legumes, but also to eliminate some of the harmful elements. It is also a good idea to cook them with the addition of aromatic herbs (bay, rosemary etc.).

First carefully clean all the earth off the truffle. Melt the butter in a saucepan, without letting it fry, remove from the heat and add 3 dessert spoons of grated parmesan cheese, mix with a small hand whisk. Season with a little freshly ground pepper and a pinch of nutmeg, then dilute with the boiling stock and the roast gravy, stirring carefully all the time. Put the saucepan back on the heat and, stirring continually, allow the sauce to boil and then simmer on a moderate heat, until it thickens. Meanwhile put a pan of water on to heat and when it boils add the salt

• Spaghetti with hare •

400 g of spaghetti, salt, 4 dessert spoons of extra virgin olive oil, 500 g of hare (thigh and breast), 1 clove of garlic, 1 sprig of rosemary, 50 g of bacon pieces, pepper, 1 glass of red wine, 2 dessert spoons of tomato passata, 4 dessert spoons of grated parmesan cheese.

Heat the oil and the butter in a saucepan, add the pieces of hare and allow to brown on quite a high heat. Then add a mix of chopped garlic, bacon and rosemary, season with a little pepper and, after a few minutes, add the red wine. Allow the liquid to evaporate then add the tomato passata, diluted in a glass of warm water, and leave to cook on a moderate heat for about 1 hour.

When it is cooked, remove the bones from the hare, chop the meat and put back in the saucepan, leave to cook for a further five minutes. Start cooking the spaghetti: boil the water, add salt and cook the pasta until al dente, drain and pour into a serving dish, sprinkle with parmesan cheese then add the sauce, stir thoroughly and serve, together with a glass of good red wine.

• Spaghetti with rabbit •

400 g of spaghetti, salt, 1 onion, 1 piece of white celery, 2 dessert spoons of extra virgin olive oil, 40 g of butter, 200 g of rabbit meat (thigh and breast), a little wholewheat flour, 1/2 a glass of white wine, pepper, 1 teaspoon of chopped thyme.

Peel and finely chop the onion; wash the carrot under running water, scrape and finely chop it; trim and wash the celery, finely chop. Then put all these in a saucepan, add the oil and almost all of
the butter and then sauté over a high heat for a few minutes. Cut the rabbit meat into bite size pieces, coat in a little flour, and add to the saucepan; allow to brown and then add the white wine, season with salt and pepper and the thyme. Cover and allow to cook for about half an hour. Put a pan of water on to heat, when it boils, add the salt and cook the spaghetti until al dente, then drain. Thoroughly mix the spaghetti with the remaining butter and the rabbit sauce. Serve.

• Spaghetti with Bolognese sauce •

400 g of spaghetti, salt, 1 small onion, 1 piece of carrot, 1 piece of celery, 100 g of beef, 100 g of bacon, 2 chicken livers, 2 ripe tomatoes, 50 g of butter, 1/2 a cup of white wine, pepper, nutmeg, 1 cup of meat stock.

SBolognese sauce is quite famous and internationally widespread and certainly needs no great introduction: it is definitely one of the classic sauces for pasta in general, and spaghetti in particular. To live up to its famous name it needs to be prepared with a little care and attention, but you don't have to be a master chef to get good results. Peel and finely chop the onion; do the same with the washed and dried carrot and the celery. Slice the bacon thinly, wash and mince the chicken livers and the beef. Plunge the tomatoes in boiling water so that the skin is easy to remove, remove the seeds and then pass the tomatoes through a sieve.

Heat the butter in a saucepan and slowly brown the chopped vegetables, the bacon, the livers and the beef, stir well and add the white wine. Then add the sieved tomatoes and season with salt and pepper and a little nutmeg, pour in the meat stock and leave to cook on a moderate heat for about 1 hour, stirring from time to time. The pasta should be cooked in the usual way: put a pan of water on to heat, when it boils add the salt and then the spaghetti. When the pasta is cooked al dente, drain it and pour into a serving dish, add the sauce. If you wish you can sprinkle with parmesan cheese before serving. If you would prefer a simplified version of this recipe exclude the chicken livers.

• Spaghetti with bacon and gorgonzola cheese •

400 g of spaghetti, salt, 15 dessert spoons of extra virgin olive oil, 1 small piece of red chilli pepper, 200 g of bacon, 200 g of mild gorgonzola cheese, 4 dl of single cream, 100 g of grated parmesan cheese.

Bacon and gorgonzola cheese: an excellent, tasty combination. The strong flavour of the bacon, especially if you use a good, tasty smoked bacon, goes perfectly with the

flavour and softness of the mild gorgonzola cheese. Heat the oil in a frying pan, add the chopped chilli pepper and the bacon, cut into matchsticks.

Allow to cook slowly so that the fat of the bacon melts and then add the cubes of gorgonzola cheese. Continue to cook slowly, stirring with a wooden spoon, until the cheese melts and coats the pieces of bacon. Lastly add the cream, in order to dilute and soften the flavour. Put a pan of water on to heat for the pasta, when it boils add the salt and cook the spaghetti until al dente.

When you have drained the spaghetti add the sauce and stir well. Serve, offering grated parmesan cheese. If you prefer you can substitute the red chilli pepper with a couple of cloves of crushed garlic.

• Spaghetti with bacon •

400 g of spaghetti, salt, 500 g of ripe tomatoes,
1 bunch of parsley, 4 cloves of garlic, 10 basil leaves,
200 g of smoked bacon, 3 dessert spoons of extra virgin olive oil,
30 g of butter (about 1 dessert spoon), 4 dessert spoons
of grated parmesan cheese.

If you can manage to get some traditionally smoked bacon then the result will be better. In any case, begin by preparing the tomatoes: plunge them into boiling water to remove the skins, then remove the seeds and chop them.
Trim, wash and dry the parsley then finely chop it, together with the cloves of garlic and the basil leaves, finely

chop the bacon. Heat the oil in a frying pan, add the bacon and allow to brown, then add the tomatoes, garlic, parsley and basil.

Season with salt and pepper and then cook for about a 1/4 of an hour on a moderate heat, stirring from time to time with a wooden spoon. In the meantime cook the spaghetti in plenty of salted, boiling water, drain when al dente and pour into a serving dish, add the butter and the grated cheese and lastly the bacon sauce.

• Spaghetti Antonia •

400 g of spaghetti, salt, 250 g of broccoli,
120 g of smoked bacon, 3 dessert spoons of extra virgin olive oil,
1 small piece of chilli pepper, 1 clove of garlic,
4 dessert spoons of grated pecorino cheese.

This recipe is also based on the use of bacon, but in this case the sauce is enriched with broccoli. You can use cauliflower, but in any case it is better to use only the florets, eliminating the leaves and the harder parts of the stalk, as they require longer cooking times.

Trim, wash and chop up the broccoli; dice the smoked bacon. Pour the oil into a frying pan and fry the bacon with the chopped chilli pepper and the garlic. Then discard the garlic and add the broccoli, season lightly with salt and continue to cook for about 25 minutes, stirring from time to time with a wooden spoon. Put a pan of water on to heat for the pasta, when it boils add the salt and cook the spaghetti, drain when al dente. Pour into a serving dish, add the sauce and the grated cheese. Serve.

• Spaghetti carbonara •

400 g of spaghetti, salt, 200 g piece of lean bacon, 1 clove of garlic, 6 dessert spoons of extra virgin olive oil, 2 eggs, 2 egg yolks, 3 dessert spoons of grated parmesan cheese, 3 dessert spoons of grated pecorino cheese, pepper.

Spaghetti carbonara has become a classic offering of traditional Mediterranean cuisine and it is without doubt quite filling, as well as very tasty.

First cut the bacon into 1/2 cm cubes and brown in a frying pan along with the oil and garlic. Remove the garlic as soon as it becomes golden brown. Beat the whole eggs in a warmed serving dish, add the two egg yolks and the grated cheese, season with salt and plenty of freshly ground pepper, mix thoroughly until creamy, make sure that it is ready as soon as the spaghetti has been cooked in plenty of salted, boiling water.

Then pour the hot spaghetti into the serving dish with the eggs, mix well, and add the hot, crispy bacon. Serve immediately.

• Spaghetti with frankfurters •

*400 g of spaghetti, salt, 8 frankfurters, 1 bunch of parsley,
40 g of butter (about 2 dessert spoons), 100 g of crescenza
cheese, a pinch of mild paprika, 2 dessert spoons of grated
emmenthal cheese, 2 dessert spoons of grated parmesan cheese.*

Frankfurters are not always made with good quality ingredients so it would be a good idea to check carefully that you are buying a product which can be trusted. In any case, begin by removing the skin and slicing them into rounds; then trim, wash and
finely chop the parsley. Melt the butter in a saucepan, add the frankfurters and, after a moment, the parsley and the crescenza, which you have creamed together with the paprika. Season lightly with salt and stir continually with a wooden spoon, cook for about 3 minutes on a moderate heat. In the meantime put a pan of water on to heat for the pasta, when it boils add the salt and cook the spaghetti. When the pasta is al dente, drain and pour into a serving dish, add the sauce and sprinkle with the grated parmesan cheese, stir well.

• Spaghetti with gravy •

*400 g of spaghetti, salt, 1 medium size onion, 1 carrot
1 celery stalk, 3 dessert spoons of extra virgin olive oil,
50 g of butter, 600 g of beef (shoulder or leg), pepper, nutmeg,
1 cup of meat stock, 4 dessert spoons of grated parmesan cheese.*

FRANKFURTERS

The first frankfurters were produced in Germany, more precisely in Frankfurt, where they took their actual form in 1903, however they were mentioned in the menu of a local restaurant in 1760, even if their origins were lost a few hundred years before. The popularity of this German speciality grew so quickly that it soon became famous all over the world. Frankfurters should be made from leg of pork, with the tendons and fat removed, it should then be minced and prepared according to an antique recipe, without any chemical additives. The mixture obtained should be then made into sausages, using sheep intestines for the skin, and smoked using a method which gives them their unique flavour. This, obviously, is the traditional way of doing things, but, as usual, in the food industry things are not always as they should be.

Peel and finely chop the onion; trim and wash the carrot, finely chop; do the same with the celery. Heat the oil and butter in a saucepan and sauté the onion, carrot and celery, then add the beef and brown evenly, season with salt and pepper and a pinch of nutmeg, then add the stock with a spoon.

Allow to stew quite slowly until most of the liquid has evaporated and the gravy has become quite rich and thick, it should form bubbles on the surface, the success of this sauce depends on the cooking and some people even prolong the cooking, on a low heat for up to five hours. Put a pan of water on to heat for the pasta, when it boils add the salt and cook the spaghetti. When al dente, drain and transfer to a suitable serving dish, add the sauce and serve offering grated parmesan cheese.

• Spaghetti with raw ham •

400 g of spaghetti, salt, 1/2 an onion, 200 g of raw ham, 50 g of butter, 3 eggs, pepper, 4 dessert spoons of grated parmesan cheese.

Peel and finely chop the onion, cut the ham into thin strips. Melt the butter in a small saucepan and add the onion, stir with a wooden spoon and allow to soften without changing colour. Next add the ham and sauté for a few minutes. Break the eggs into a bowl, add a pinch of salt and a little freshly ground pepper, add the grated cheese and beat with a fork until frothy.

Put a pan of water on to heat, when it boils, add the salt and cook the spaghetti, drain when al dente. Put the eggs and the ham together in a large non-stick frying pan, add the spaghetti and heat for a few minutes on a high heat, stirring continually with a wooden spoon until the egg sets then serve immediately.

• Spaghetti with ham •

*400 g of spaghetti, salt, 40 g of butter, 1/2 an onion,
1 clove of garlic, 1 medium size Rennet apple, 1 dessert spoon
of wholewheat flour, pepper, 2 dessert spoons of Cognac,
4 dessert spoons of cream, 4 dessert spoons of grated parmesan
cheese, 150 g of boiled ham.*

Spaghetti with ham is characterised not only by the use of
cooked ham, but also by the use of a Rennet apple, which
gives this dish an unusual, pleasant flavour. First peel the
apple, remove the core and slice thinly; peel the onion
and the garlic too. Melt the butter in a saucepan and add
the finely chopped onion and garlic, after a few moments
add the slices of apple, the flour and a little salt and pepper. Stir with a wooden spoon and cook for about ten
minutes, on a moderate heat, before adding the Cognac,
allow to evaporate then add the cream and the parmesan
cheese. Put a pan of water on to heat, when it boils add
the salt and cook the spaghetti, drain when cooked. Pour
the spaghetti into a serving dish, add the sauce and the
ham, cut into thin strips.

• Spaghetti amatriciana •

400 g of spaghetti, salt, 200 g piece of bacon,
6 dessert spoons of extra virgin olive oil, 1/2 an onion,
300 g of firm ripe tomatoes, a small piece of chilli pepper,
4 dessert spoons of grated pecorino cheese.

Amatriciana is, without doubt, one of the most famous pasta sauces: the original recipe did not include tomatoes and so it is possible to avoid using them, or to use a smaller quantity. Cut the bacon into cubes then brown in the oil: as soon as the fat melts remove the bacon from the pan and keep on one side.

Add the finely chopped onion to the same pan and sauté, then add the tomatoes, which you have previously plunged in hot water to remove the skins, de-seeded and cut into strips. Season with salt and leave to simmer for about ten minutes, until the sauce thickens, then add the bacon and the piece of chilli pepper, or, if you prefer, some chilli powder.

Put a pan of water on to heat for the pasta, when it boils add the salt and cook the spaghetti. When it is cooked al dente drain it and transfer to a serving dish, add the sauce. Lastly, sprinkle with grated pecorino cheese and serve.

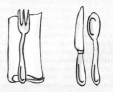

• Spaghetti with salami •

400 g of spaghetti, salt, 50 g of butter, 200 g of smoked salami, 250 g of tinned tomatoes, 1/2 a glass of cream, pepper, 2 egg yolks, 4 dessert spoons of grated parmesan cheese.

Melt the butter in a saucepan and add the salami, cut into thin strips. Leave to cook for 5 minutes on a moderate heat, then add the tomatoes and leave on the heat for a further 1/4 of an hour.

Put a pan of water on to heat, when it boils add the salt and cook the spaghetti. When it is al dente drain the spaghetti and pour it into a serving dish, add the cream, freshly ground pepper and the egg yolks, stir well then add the grated parmesan cheese and the salami sauce, stir again, thoroughly and serve.

• Spaghetti with rosemary •

400 g of spaghetti, salt, 1 clove of garlic, 40 g of butter, 300 g of beef, 1/2 a glass of dry white wine, 2 dessert spoons of chopped rosemary needles, 2 cloves, 250 g of tinned tomatoes, pepper, 50 g of grated parmesan cheese.

This rosemary sauce is very easy to make: however it requires quite a long cooking time, at least an hour on a low heat, so before beginning ensure that you have enough time available.

Peel the garlic clove and brown in the melted butter, then

discard it and substitute with the minced beef. Brown on a high heat then add the white wine, when the wine has evaporated add the rosemary, the cloves and the tomatoes. Wet everything with a cup of water, season, cover, and cook for about 1 hour on a moderate heat, stirring from time to time with a wooden spoon. Then put a pan of water on to heat, when it boils add the salt and cook the spaghetti until al dente. Then drain and pour into a serving dish, add the sauce and the grated parmesan cheese. Stir thoroughly.

• Spaghetti
with sausage and mushrooms •

400 g of spaghetti, salt, 3 medium size, firm, ripe tomatoes, 250 g of button mushrooms, 1/2 an onion, 1 bunch of parsley, 3 dessert spoons of extra virgin olive oil, 1 clove of garlic, 200 g of sausage meat, a piece of chilli pepper or chilli powder, 3 dessert spoons of grated parmesan cheese.

Put a pan of water on to heat, when it boils plunge the tomatoes into the water so that their skins come away easily; then remove their seeds and put them through a vegetable mill. Next clean the mushrooms, wash them under cold running water, dry them and slice them thinly; peel and finely chop the onion.
Heat the oil in a frying pan and sauté the onion, add the finely chopped, or crushed, garlic; add the mushrooms and

a little chopped parsley and allow to cook, on quite a high heat, for a few minutes. Then add the finely chopped sausage and carry on cooking, stirring continually. After 5 minutes add the tomatoes and the chilli pepper and leave to cook for a further 1/4 of an hour, lowering the heat slightly.

Put a large pan of water on to heat, when it boils add the salt and the spaghetti. When it is cooked drain the spaghetti and pour it into a serving dish, add the sauce and sprinkle with chopped parsley, a few whole parsley leaves and a little grated parmesan cheese. You can also add a little olive oil if you wish.

Obviously in the recipe we advise the use of cultivated button mushrooms, because these are the most readily available: but if you can use woodland or wild mushrooms the result would, undoubtedly, be much better.

• Spaghetti with sausage •

400 g of spaghetti, salt, 1 medium size onion, 1 celery stalk, 1 carrot, 1 clove of garlic, 2 dessert spoons of extra virgin olive oil, 50 g of butter, 200 g sausages, 1 dessert spoon of tomato puree, 1 bunch of parsley, 4 dessert spoons of grated parmesan cheese.

Sanyone who loves sausages won't regret making this tasty sausage spaghetti sauce. Peel the onion, trim and wash the celery, trim the carrot and scrub it under cold running water, peel the garlic. Dry the vegetables that have been

washed and then chop them all very finely. Heat the oil and half of the butter in a saucepan, add the finely chopped vegetables, sauté on a high heat, stirring with a wooden spoon, skin the sausage and break into small pieces, add to the vegetables.

Brown for a few minutes, then add a cup of hot water, in which you have dissolved the tomato puree, and then leave to cook, on a moderate heat for at least an hour, or until the sauce has thickened considerably. Put a pan of water on to heat for the spaghetti, when it boils add the salt and cook the pasta.

When it is al dente drain the spaghetti and pour it into a serving dish, add the sauce, the remaining butter, the chopped parsley and grated cheese. Serve immediately.

• Spaghetti carrettiera •

400 g of spaghetti, salt, 8 dessert spoons of extra virgin olive oil, 2 cloves of garlic, 60 g of bacon, 250 g of cep mushrooms, pepper, 80 g of tuna in oil, 3 dl of gravy, 100 g of grated parmesan cheese.

Peel and finely chop the garlic, heat the oil in a frying pan and add the garlic. As soon as the garlic begins to brown add the chopped bacon and the mushrooms which have been washed, dried and sliced.

Season to taste and cook for a few minutes, stir and then add the crumbled up tuna, leave to cook on a moderate heat until every thing is nicely blended. Put a pan of water on to heat for the spaghetti, when it boils add the salt and cook the pasta. Drain the spaghetti when it is al dente then pour it into a serving dish. Add the sauce that you prepared previously and some gravy, serve offering grated parmesan cheese. You can use any gravy that you have already or you can prepare some by cooking a piece of beef for a long time with oil, onion and herbs.

• Spaghetti cacciatora •

400 g of spaghetti, salt, 500 g of wild boar meat, wholewheat flour, 80 g of extra virgin olive oil, 2 cloves of garlic, 1 piece of rosemary, pepper, 30 g of dried mushrooms, a glass of red wine, 50 g of tomato puree.

Spaghetti Cacciatora can be prepared with wild boar as well as venison or goat. First cut the meat into cubes and coat it in flour. Then heat the oil in a frying pan and add the crushed garlic: leave the pan on the heat for a moment then discard the garlic, substitute it with the rosemary and then add the cubes of meat.

Allow the meat to brown then check the gravy and season to taste. Soak the dried mushrooms in a little warm water then chop roughly and add to the meat. Leave everything to cook for a few minutes, so the flavours can mingle, then pour in the wine, allow to evaporate and then add the tomato puree, diluted with a little warm water.

Leave to finish cooking on a moderate heat, if the sauce seems to be drying up too quickly add a little warm water. Put a pan of water on to heat for the pasta, when it boils add the salt and cook the spaghetti. When it is al dente, drain and pour into a serving dish, add the sauce and serve.

• Spaghetti pizzaiola •

*400 g of spaghetti, salt, 1 teaspoon of salted capers,
a few sprigs of parsley, 3 firm, ripe tomatoes, 350 g of beef,
2 cloves of garlic, 4 dessert spoons of extra virgin olive oil,
oregano, a small piece of chilli pepper, 5 dessert spoons
of grated parmesan cheese.*

Wash the capers in cold water and squeeze them; wash the parsley. In the meantime put a pan of water on to heat, when it boils plunge the tomatoes into the water for a moment so that the skin comes off easily; remove the seeds and put the tomatoes through a vegetable mill. Cut the meat into thin strips. Pour the oil into a frying pan and heat, crush the garlic and fry in the oil: when it begins to change colour remove it from the oil.

Put the meat into the pan, add the tomatoes and allow to cook on a moderate heat, stirring occasionally. Now add the capers, the oregano, the finely chopped chilli pepper and some leaves of parsley, season with salt and simmer for about half an hour, stirring from time to time with a wooden spoon.

Put a pan with plenty of water on to heat, when it boils add the salt and cook the spaghetti. When the spaghetti is cooked, drain it and transfer it to a serving dish, add the sauce and sprinkle with the grated cheese and a few leaves of parsley.

• Spaghetti with chicken livers •

400 g of spaghetti, salt, 200 g of chicken livers, a little wholewheat flour, 1 small onion, 50 g of butter, 1/2 a glass of white wine, pepper, grated parmesan cheese.

The preparation of this sauce, using chicken livers, is not at all difficult: it is quite quick to make and the only thing which needs a little extra care and attention is the cleaning of the livers. So, begin by trimming them well and removing the fat, wash them, dry them with a clean cloth and chop them into small pieces, coat the pieces lightly in flour. Peel and finely chop the onion, melt the butter in a frying pan and sauté the onion until golden brown, then add the livers. Stir with a wooden spoon and sprinkle with the white wine and fry for another 3-4 minutes, then season with salt and a little pepper.

Put a pan of water on to heat for the spaghetti, when it boils add the salt and cook the pasta. When it is al dente drain it and pour it into a serving dish, add the chicken liver sauce. Serve immediately, offering grated parmesan cheese.

• Spaghetti arrabbiata •

400 g of spaghetti, salt, 400 g of mixed pork offal,
1/2 a glass of extra virgin olive oil, 4 cloves of garlic,
red chilli powder, pepper, 50 g of sultanas, 10 walnuts,
2 glasses of white wine, a handful of grated pecorino cheese.

Spaghetti arrabbiata is a decidedly spicy dish, suitable for quite a strong stomach, it can, without doubt be offered as a filling main course. First trim and wash the offal and then mince it; then cook in a frying pan with the oil and the crushed garlic, adding a generous pinch of red chilli powder and some pepper. Keep stirring, meanwhile leave the sultanas to soak in a little warm water.

After about ten minutes cooking add the drained sultanas to the offal, add the shelled and finely chopped walnuts and the white wine, so that you obtain a thick but abundant sauce. Simmer, stirring from time to time with a wooden spoon, when cooked put through a blender and then put back in the pan to keep warm.

Put a pan of water on to heat for the spaghetti, when it boils add the salt and cook the pasta until al dente. Then drain it and sprinkle with the pecorino cheese, pour it into the pan with the sauce and heat for about 5 minutes, but not on too high a heat.

Finally pour into a warmed serving dish, sprinkle with freshly ground pepper and serve, accompanied by a good red wine.

• Recipes with fish •

Spaghetti sauces made with fish are suitable for all seasons but, perhaps, above all for summer. Clams, mussels, cuttlefish, squid, tuna, anchovies, sardines, herrings, caviar, lobster, scampi etc. There is just so much to choose from; in some cases some of the recipes are a little complicated, but most of them require very little hard work and so are suitable for anyone who doesn't have a lot of time to dedicate to cooking.

• Spaghetti with clams •

*400 g of spaghetti, salt, 1 kg of clams, extra virgin olive oil,
2 cloves of garlic, 1 red chilli pepper,
dry white wine (optional), 1 bunch of parsley.*

The clam is a very well known shellfish. The striped, fan-shaped shell is no more than 4-6 cm long. This delicate flavoured shellfish should only be eaten raw if its origins are safe. This clam sauce doesn't require any complicated elaboration; but as it isn't sieved it is important to clean the clams very carefully before cooking, so as to avoid having sand in the sauce.

Clean the shells under running water and then leave them to soak, for at least half an hour in salted water, so that any sand trapped between the valves is eliminated.

When the clams have been soaked put them in a frying pan with plenty of oil, 1 sliced garlic clove, the chilli pepper and, if you wish, some white wine.

Cover the pan and allow the clams to open on quite a high heat. In the meantime put a pan of water on to heat for the pasta: when the water boils add the salt and cook the spaghetti, drain when al dente.

Pour the spaghetti into the pan with the clams and stir with a wooden spoon, heat on quite a high heat, sprinkle with a mix of finely chopped parsley and garlic. Serve with a good, cold white wine.

• Spaghetti with clams and tomato •

*400 g of spaghetti, salt, 1/2 a glass of extra virgin olive oil,
2 cloves of garlic, 500 g of chopped tomatoes, 1 small piece
of chilli pepper, 500 g of clams, 1 bunch of parsley.*

Heat the oil in a large frying pan, add the peeled garlic
cloves and when they begin to change colour discard
them, add the chopped tomatoes to the pan.
Allow to cook for a few minutes on a high heat and then
lower, season with a little salt and the piece of chilli pepper. Meanwhile wash the clams very carefully and leave
them for at least half an hour in salted water, so that they
lose any sand that is trapped between the valves. When
the tomato sauce has thickened add the clams.
Put a pan of water on to heat for the pasta and when it
boils cook the spaghetti until al dente. Drain and pour into
the pan with the clams, sprinkle with chopped parsley and
stir for a few minutes on a moderate heat, so that all the
flavours can mingle. Serve directly from the pan.

• Spaghetti with mussels •

*400 g of spaghetti, salt, 800 g of mussels, 2 cloves of garlic,
some parsley, a piece of yellow or red pepper,
4 dessert spoons of extra virgin olive oil.*

Also with this sauce the most difficult part is cleaning the
mussels thoroughly enough to eliminate any sand that

could be trapped between the valves. So, wash the mussels very carefully in cold water and then cook them in a frying pan, with a little water, on a high heat.

As soon as they open remove the pan from the heat, detach the mussels from their shells and sieve the cooking water. Then peel and finely chop the garlic, trim, wash, dry and finely chop the parsley too.

Pour the oil into a frying pan and sauté the chopped garlic; add the finely chopped chilli powder and the mussels, stir with a wooden spoon and add a little of the mussels' cooking liquor, stir again, add the chopped parsley and cook for a couple of minutes more. In the meantime put a pan of water on to cook the spaghetti: when the water boils add the salt and cook the pasta until al dente, then drain. Pour the spaghetti into the pan with the mussels, add a little olive oil, stir thoroughly and serve.

• Spaghetti with sepia •

*400 g of fine spaghetti, salt, 400 g of small cuttlefish
and a few sacks of sepia, 1 clove of garlic, 4 dessert spoons
of extra virgin olive oil, 5 medium size ripe tomatoes,
1 bunch of parsley, red chilli powder.*

Thoroughly and carefully trim and wash the cuttlefish then roughly chop them. Pour the oil into a frying pan and sauté the finely chopped garlic, then add the cuttlefish and a ladle of water and allow to cook for a 1/4 of an hour before adding the tomatoes, which have been plunged in boiling water to remove the skins, de-seeded and then roughly chopped. In the meantime put a pan of water on to heat for the pasta: when the water boils add the salt and cook the spaghetti.

When the sauce has become quite thick break the ink sacks into the frying pan and sprinkle with chopped parsley, salt and chilli powder. Allow to cook for a little longer so that the flavours can mingle then add the drained spaghetti and cook for another two minutes before serving. There is a version of this recipe that does not include tomatoes; in that case you can cook the cuttlefish with the help of a little white wine or a few ladles of hot stock.

• Spaghetti with cuttlefish •

400 g of spaghetti, salt, 500 g of small, delicate cuttlefish, 1/2 a glass of extra virgin olive oil, 1 medium size onion, pepper, a bunch of parsley.

Clean the cuttlefish, removing the bone, the eyes and the ink sacks. Wash them thoroughly then cut off the tentacles and divide them into small pieces, cut the bodies into strips. Next, heat the oil in a frying pan, add the peeled and finely chopped onion and the pieces of tentacle, allow to soften and then add the strips of cuttlefish.

Season with salt and pepper then allow to finish cooking on a moderate heat, adding a couple of tablespoons of warm water if necessary.

When the sauce is cooked add the washed, dried and fine-

ly chopped parsley. Put a pan of water on to heat for the pasta and, when it begins to boil, add the salt and the spaghetti. Cook until al dente, drain and pour into a serving dish, stir in the sauce.

As for variations of this recipe, you can enrich the sauce a little by adding a little celery, carrot and rosemary to the onion, you could also give the oil more flavour by using a couple of finely chopped or crushed garlic cloves instead of the onion. Lastly you could also add some chopped, pureed tomatoes, which should be allowed to cook together with the cuttlefish; in this case you could use a little less cuttlefish.

• Spaghetti with salmon •

400 g of spaghetti, salt, 100 g of natural tinned salmon,
4 dessert spoons of extra virgin olive oil, a bunch of parsley,
1 dessert spoon of salted capers.

This salmon sauce is quick and easy to make: you can use tinned salmon, as long as it is good quality, so that the sauce is suitable to be served on any occasion. First drain the liquid off the salmon and break it into flakes using a fork. Heat the oil in a small saucepan, add the salmon, season with salt and a little pepper, allow to cook for a few minutes on a moderate heat.

In the meantime put a pan of water on to heat for the pasta, when it boils add the salt and the spaghetti. Trim and wash the parsley, then finely chop together with the rinsed capers, add this mix to the salmon a few seconds before removing from the heat.

When the spaghetti is cooked al dente, drain it and pour it into a serving dish, add the salmon sauce, stir well and serve immediately, accompanied by a good, cold white wine.

• Spaghetti
with smoked salmon •

400 g of spaghetti, salt, 1 spring onion, 10 walnuts,
50 g of shelled pistachio nuts, 8 dessert spoons
of extra virgin olive oil, cognac, 200 g of sliced,
smoked salmon, pepper, 1 egg yolk.

Heat 5 dessert spoons of oil in a frying pan and sauté the washed, finely chopped spring onion, together with the roughly chopped walnuts and pistachios. After a few minutes add a drop of cognac and allow to evaporate, then add the salmon, cut into strips and a little freshly ground pepper; cook for a few minutes on quite a high heat and then remove from the heat.

Put a pan of water on to heat for the pasta, when it boils add the salt and the spaghetti. In the meantime beat the eggs, in a serving dish, with 3 dessert spoons of olive oil and a pinch of salt.

When the spaghetti is cooked al dente, drain it and pour it into a serving dish, add the salmon sauce, stir well and serve. Variations of this recipe suggest using a 1/4 litre of cream instead of the egg yolk, obviously the choice is yours.

• Spaghetti marinara •

400 g of spaghetti, salt, 100 g of green olives, 8 fresh anchovies, 1 bunch of parsley, 1 clove of garlic, 5 dessert spoons of extra virgin olive oil, 1 small piece of red chilli pepper, 350 g of ripe tomatoes, 4 dessert spoons of grated parmesan cheese.

Spaghetti marinara is a decidedly tasty and appetising dish, it is quite easy to make and needs just a few cheap ingredients. Which doesn't hurt! Remove the stones and roughly chop the olives; wash the anchovies under running water, remove the heads and the bones and cut the fish into small pieces; trim the parsley, wash, dry and chop finely. Brown the garlic in a small saucepan with the oil, then eliminate it and add the anchovies, the olives, the parsley and a small piece of chilli pepper to the oil.

Cook for a few minutes on a moderate heat then add the tomatoes, which have been peeled, de-seeded and roughly chopped, season with salt and continue cooking for about twenty minutes, stirring from time to time with a wooden spoon. Put a pan of water on to heat for the pasta; when it boils add the salt and cook the spaghetti until al dente. Drain well and pour into a serving dish, just before serving sprinkle with the grated cheese and add the sauce.

• Spaghetti with herring •

400 g of spaghetti, salt, 2 dessert spoons of extra virgin olive oil, 1 clove of garlic, 250 g of peeled plum tomatoes, a few sprigs of parsley, pepper, 200 g of smoked herring fillets.

Even nowadays, in some areas of Italy, herring is considered a food to be eaten on particular occasions: on some holidays, at the end of Carnival time, on "fasting" days etc. So a spaghetti sauce made with this fish is quite appreciated. Heat the oil in a small saucepan and add the whole garlic clove; when it begins to brown discard it, and add the tomatoes, which have been squashed with a fork.

Wash the parsley leaves and add them to the tomatoes, season with a pinch of salt and some freshly ground pepper. Cook on quite a high heat for 5 minutes, then add the chopped herring, lower the heat and continue to cook for about half an hour, or until the sauce has thickened. Then put a pan of water on to heat for the pasta and, when it boils, add the salt and the spaghetti. Cook until al dente then drain and put in a serving dish, add the herring sauce. Serve after having stirred thoroughly.

• Spaghetti with fresh anchovies •

400 g of spaghetti, salt, 200 g of very fresh anchovies, 2 cloves of garlic, 1 bunch of parsley, 40 g of breadcrumbs, 4 dessert spoons of extra virgin olive oil, juice of 1/2 a lemon.

This anchovy sauce can also be made with a few, cheap ingredients. It needs just a little care and attention when cleaning the fish, but this is by no means difficult.

Clean the fish, remove the heads, tails and bones: wash the fillets very carefully under running water, then chop them quite roughly and put them in a saucepan with a mix of garlic and parsley, both finely chopped, the breadcrumbs and the oil. Leave on quite a high heat for a few minutes, stirring with a wooden spoon until the anchovies are tender and the breadcrumbs are golden brown.

Then put a pan of water on to heat for the pasta and, when it boils, add the salt and the spaghetti.

Cook until al dente then drain and put in a serving dish, sprinkle with the strained lemon juice, mix carefully and then add the anchovy sauce, stir again and serve.

• Spaghetti ammiraglia •

400 g of spaghetti, salt, 1/2 a glass of extra virgin olive oil,
3 cloves of garlic, 1 small piece of red chilli pepper,
100 g of herrings in oil, pepper.

Heat the oil in a frying pan, add the finely chopped cloves of garlic and, when they begin to brown, add the chopped chilli pepper and the crumbled herring fillets. Stir with a wooden spoon, and add a couple of tablespoons of warm water to dilute the sauce a little so that it doesn't fry, add a pinch of pepper.

Now the sauce is ready, so you can begin cooking the pasta. Put a pan of water on to heat, when it boils add a little salt and the spaghetti. Cook until al dente then drain, pour into a serving dish and add the herring sauce, don't forget to serve this dish with a good, cold white wine. Because, as you know, herrings are quite salty so it is likely that you'll end up feeling very thirsty!

• Spaghetti
with truffle and anchovies •

400 g of spaghetti, salt, 4 salted anchovies, 3 small black
truffles, extra virgin olive oil, 1 clove of garlic, pepper.

The combination of anchovies and truffle makes this spaghetti sauce really tasty. Also, it is quite easy to make and takes very little time. Wash the anchovies under running water to remove the salt, then remove the bones, keeping the fillets on one side. Now thoroughly clean the truffles getting rid of all the earth, then use a pestle and mortar to make them into a smooth paste.

Heat a little oil in a saucepan and add the anchovy fillets, allow them to dissolve, stirring with a wooden spoon, add the crushed garlic, avoid browning, add the truffle, salt and a little pepper. In the meantime put a large pan of water on to heat, when it boils add the salt and the spaghetti. Cook until al dente and then drain, add the anchovy and truffle sauce and serve.

• Spaghetti with sardines •

400 g of spaghetti, salt, 6 sardines, 6 dessert spoons of extra virgin olive oil, 2 dessert spoons of tomato passata, pepper.

This is another quick and easy sauce to make. Lightly descale the sardines, cut off the heads, the gills and remove the bones, then wash under running water, dry thoroughly and chop finely.

Heat the oil in a small saucepan, add the sardines and cook on a moderate heat for 5 minutes, then add the tomato, a pinch of salt and a little pepper, leave to cook for a few minutes more, so that the sauce can thicken. Put the pan on for the pasta, and when the water begins to boil add the salt and the spaghetti. Cook until al dente, drain and pour into a serving dish, add the sauce and serve.

• Spaghetti with anchovies •

400 g of spaghetti, salt, 7 anchovy fillets, 100 g of fontina cheese, 3 egg yolks, 20 g of butter (approx. 1 dessert spoon), pepper.

Break the anchovy fillets up with a fork, then chop the fontina cheese into small pieces. Beat the egg yolks and the cheese, together in a bowl then leave the mixture to rest for a while. In the meantime melt the butter, in a frying pan, on a very low heat, then add the egg and cheese mixture and the pieces of anchovy, stir well.

Put a pan on to heat for the pasta and, when the water begins to boil add the salt and the spaghetti.

Cook until al dente, drain and pour into the frying pan with the sauce. Leave on the heat for a moment, stirring with a wooden spoon and, after having sprinkled with freshly ground pepper, serve.

An simplified version of this recipe entails browning a few cloves of garlic in oil, then adding the chopped anchovy fillets, and leaving to cook for a few minutes.

You can then add this sauce to the spaghetti, with a generous sprinkling of chopped parsley.

Usually more anchovies are used in this recipe than in the one with cheese and eggs, so you might find that you could do with a good, cold white wine or even a jug of cold water to quench your thirst.

• Spaghetti with caviar - 1 •

400 g of spaghetti, salt, 1 large onion,
2 dessert spoons of extra virgin olive oil, 100 g of butter,
1/4 of a glass of dry white wine, 50 g of caviar,
4 dessert spoons of grated emmenthal cheese.

Peel and finely chop the onion, put it into a frying pan with the oil and the butter and sauté on a moderate heat, stirring with a wooden spoon. Then add the white wine, cover and cook for a few more minutes.

Put a pan of water on to heat for the pasta, when it boils add the salt and the spaghetti. Drain and pour into the frying pan, add the caviar, stir and heat for a moment, season with salt to taste, sprinkle with the grated cheese and serve.

• Spaghetti with caviar - 2 •

400 g of spaghetti, salt, 50 g of butter, 1 dl of single cream
pepper, 60 g of caviar.

Here is another recipe for a spaghetti sauce based on caviar: in this one the preparation is also very simple and you could use a relatively lower quality caviar, with a stronger flavour. First put a pan on to heat for the pasta and, when the water boils, add the salt and the spaghetti. In the meantime melt the butter in a frying pan and add the cream, a pinch of salt and some freshly ground pepper. Cook just long enough for the flavours to mingle, then add the caviar and stir a couple of times with a wooden spoon.

When the pasta is cooked al dente drain it and pour it into the pan with the caviar sauce, stir well and serve. If you prefer, you could add a spoonful of roast gravy to the sauce, or a few spoonfuls of grated parmesan cheese. This combined with the caviar, strange as it may seem, is not at all unpleasant.

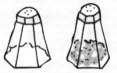

• Spaghetti and prawns •

400 g of spaghetti, salt, 250 g of prawns, 1 ripe tomato, 1 clove of garlic, a few fresh basil leaves, 4 dessert spoons of extra virgin olive oil, a small glass of brandy, pepper.

Obviously you can use ready cooked prawns, especially if you are in a hurry, but the best results will be obtained by buying fresh prawns and cooking them at home, besides it is not difficult or particularly complicated. So the first thing to do is wash the prawns and cook them in boiling water for 4 minutes.

Then drain the prawns and plunge the tomato in a pan of boiling water, so that after cooling for a moment, the skin

can easily be removed. Chop the tomato. Peel and finely chop the garlic, chop the basil; pour the oil into a frying pan and heat, brown the garlic, then add the brandy before adding the tomato, basil, a little salt and a pinch of pepper. After having added all these ingredients allow to cook on quite a moderate heat and, when the sauce has thickened, add the prawns.

Put a pan of water on to heat for the pasta and, when the water boils, add the spaghetti. Cook until al dente, then drain and pour into the pan with the sauce, stir with a wooden spoon and allow to heat for a moment before serving.

• Spaghetti with botargo •

*400 g of spaghetti, salt, about 10 dessert spoons
of extra virgin olive oil, 1 clove of garlic, 120 g of tuna,
1/2 a glass of dry white wine, 200 g of ripe tomatoes,
30 g of botargo, a bunch of parsley.*

Botargo is made from fish roe, which is pressed and dried in a sausage shape, usually it is eaten sliced very thinly and drizzled with oil, to soften the flavour and the consistency. The most delicate botargo is made from mullet roe, but it is quite rare; it is much easier to buy botargo made of tuna roe, which has a spicier flavour.

It is considered one of the prides of Sardinian cuisine, as well as being a popular tradition in Sicily, Carloforte, a delightful little island just west of Cagliari, has become famous for producing the best botargo. So heat the oil in a frying pan with the peeled and finely chopped garlic.

As soon as the garlic begins to turn brown add the crumbled up tuna and leave on the heat for a few minutes, then add the white wine and wait for it to evaporate. Then add the pureed tomatoes and the crumbled botargo, stir once, with a wooden spoon, and add the chopped parsley. If you use botargo made from tuna roe you can use a little less than the quantity indicated in this recipe: and don't forget that it must only give a little flavour, and certainly must not dominate the other flavours.

Put a pan of water on to heat for the pasta; when the water begins to boil add the salt and the spaghetti. Cook until al dente then drain and pour into a serving dish, add the botargo sauce and serve, accompanied by a bottle of good white wine.

• Spaghetti with squid •

400 g of spaghetti, salt, 500 g of spinach,
200 g of mushrooms, extra virgin olive oil, pepper,
4-5 squid (500 g in all), 1 bunch of parsley, 1 egg, 2 dessert
spoons of grated parmesan cheese, 2 dessert spoons
of breadcrumbs, 1 clove of garlic,
500 g of firm, ripe tomatoes, red chilli powder.

The preparation of this dish requires a certain amount of time and attention, so it is advisable to begin only if you are feeling particularly inspired and confident, or on a special occasion. First trim and carefully wash the spinach, then boil in a little salted water, drain when cooked. Trim the mushrooms, wash and dry then slice, sauté them in a few spoonfuls of oil, season with salt and pepper and then finely chop them together with the drained and squeezed spinach. Now clean the squid; separate the tentacles from the bodies, discard the insides, careful not to break the ink sacks, then finely chop the tentacles and add to the mushrooms and spinach, along with a little chopped parsley, the egg, the parmesan cheese, the breadcrumbs, salt and pepper. Mix carefully until smooth, use this mixture to fill the bodies of the squid, closing them with kitchen string. Plunge the tomatoes into boiling water, so that the skin can easily be removed, then de-seed and roughly chop them. Heat a few spoonfuls of oil in a frying pan and add the crushed garlic clove, as soon as the garlic browns discard it and add the tomatoes to the oil.

When the sauce begins to simmer add the squid, salt and a little pepper; cover and cook for about 30-40 minutes, then remove the squid from the pan and keep on one side, with a few spoonfuls of the sauce.

Meanwhile put a pan of water on to heat for the pasta; when the water boils add the spaghetti, cook until al dente then drain. Put the spaghetti into the pan with the sauce and heat for a moment, sprinkle with chopped parsley and, if desired a little olive oil. Serve the spaghetti topped with the sliced squid and the remaining sauce.

• Spaghetti with scampi •

*400 g of spaghetti, salt, 400 g of quite small scampi,
1/2 a glass of extra virgin olive oil, 1 clove of garlic, red chilli
powder, the juice and rind of 1 lemon, 1 bunch of parsley.*

This scampi sauce presents no particular difficulties. To appreciate this dish, though, it must be prepared and served immediately; so use the cooking time of the spaghetti to prepare the sauce. Wash and dry the scampi and cut in half lengthways.

Heat the oil in a large frying pan and add the crushed garlic, as soon as it browns discard the garlic and add the scampi. Season with a little salt and a pinch of red chilli powder, leave to cook for about ten minutes, turn the scampi over every so often.

In the meantime the water should be heating for the pasta, when it boils add the salt and the spaghetti, cook until al dente and drain. Pour the pasta into the pan with the scampi, add the lemon juice and the yellow part of the lemon rind, cut into thin strips, and a handful of chopped parsley. Stir thoroughly and serve immediately.

• Dressings
with aromatic oils •

It can certainly be very useful to have some
home-made aromatic oils for adding to your
spaghetti dishes: they are available in an
emergency and can add a special touch to many
dishes. They are very easy to prepare, and there
are only a few rules to follow to obtain very
good results: mix the ingredients in glass
containers, choose good quality extra virgin
olive oil and use fresh herbs, preferably picked
in the early morning on a cloudy day. You can
be as adventurous as you like and experiment
with all kinds of ingredients, using the aromatic
oils that you make, not only on pasta
but to dress salads, vegetables, fish and other
cereals etc. The oil should be kept in small,
labelled bottles, preferably of dark glass,
or at least kept in a dark place.
Light can damage the quality of the oil.

• Oil with chilli peppers •

1 litre of extra virgin olive oil, 3 or 4 red chilli peppers,
1 bay leaf.

This oil is destined to become more and more spicy, due to the large quantity of chilli pepper used. It is prepared by placing the chilli peppers and the bay leaf in an airtight container and covering with the oil. It is then left to infuse, for about a month, in a cool, dark place, after which it must be filtered: if a spicier flavour is required then simply leave the oil to infuse for longer, whilst if you prefer a milder flavour dilute with fresh oil.

• Oil with basil •

1 litre of extra virgin olive oil, 1 handful of basil flower heads,
10 basil leaves.

Pick the basil flower heads in the morning, leave them to dry if they are wet with dew, and then place them in an airtight container. Then add the oil, seal and leave for 3 weeks in a cool dark place. Then add the basil leaves and leave for another week. At the end of which, the oil should be filtered and put into little bottles.

• Oil with thyme •

1 litre of extra virgin olive oil, 1 sprig of thyme,
10 white pepper corns.

If necessary wash the thyme under running water and leave it to dry in the open air. When it is completely dry put it in the bottom of an airtight container with the pepper, cover with oil and seal, leave in a cool, dark place for 3 weeks. Then filter the oil and put into bottles.

• Oil with garlic and chilli pepper •

1 litre of extra virgin olive oil, 1 red hot chilli pepper,
2 cloves of garlic.

Break the chilli pepper into small pieces, peel and thinly slice the garlic. Then put these in an airtight container and cover with oil, seal and leave in a cool, dark place for about twenty days. Then filter and put into bottles.

• Oil with spices •

1 litre of extra virgin olive oil, 2 bay leaves, 3 cloves,
3 black pepper corns, 4 juniper berries, a piece of cinnamon,
a small piece of lemon rind.

Put all the ingredients in an airtight container and add the oil. Leave to infuse for about a month, then filter and put into small bottles. This is a very good dressing.

• Oil with rosemary, sage, red chilli pepper and garlic •

1 litre of extra virgin olive oil, 2 cloves of garlic, a sprig of rosemary, a few leaves of sage, a whole red chilli pepper.

Peel the garlic cloves and put them in an airtight container, add the rosemary, the sage and the chopped chilli pepper, cover with oil and leave in a cool, dark place for about twenty days. Then filter and put into small bottles, it is now ready to use.

• Oil with garlic •

1 litre of extra virgin olive oil, 6 large, fresh cloves of garlic or 4 mature cloves of garlic.

Remove the thin film that covers the garlic cloves and flatten them slightly with the side of a knife, put them in an airtight container and cover with oil. Place in a cool, dark place for about twenty days. Filter and put in bottles.

• Oil with garlic and rosemary •

litre of extra virgin olive oil, 2-3 sprigs of rosemary,
2 cloves of garlic, rock salt, a few peppercorns.

Carefully remove the leaves from the sprig of rosemary, peel the garlic and finely chop together with the leaves of rosemary. Put these in an airtight container along with the salt and the peppercorns, add the oil, seal carefully before leaving in a cool, dark place for about a month. Filter before use, and put in small bottles.

• Oil with parsley •

Parsley, extra virgin olive oil.

This aromatic oil is very easy to prepare, it is simply a question of washing the parsley and drying it very carefully. Then you must cut it up into smaller sprigs and put it into small glass jars, pressing down slightly.
Then cover with oil and seal hermetically, keep in a cool, dark place.

• Bibliography •

AA.VV., *Salse sughi e intingoli*, La Casa Verde, Bussolengo (VR), 1993.

Buonassisi Vincenzo, *Piccolo codice della pasta*, Rizzoli, Milano, 1973.

Mayr Christoph, *Spaghetti Risotto & Tortellini*, Athesia, Bolzano, 1993.

Prandoni Michela, *100 sughi per la pasta*, Guidacucina, Milano, 1989.

Pedrotti Walter, *La pasta integrale in cucina*, Demetra, Bussolengo (VR), 1989.

Pedrotti Walter, *Conoscere e cucinare i cereali*, La Casa Verde, Bussolengo (VR), 1991.

Pedrotti Walter, *Ricette al tartufo bianco e nero*, Demetra, Bussolengo (VR), 1993.

Pedrotti Walter, *Olio extravergine d'oliva*, Demetra, Bussolengo (VR), 1993.

Valnet Jean, *Fitoterapia - Cura delle malattie con le piante*, Martello - Giunti, Firenze, 1976.

Valnet Jean, *Cura delle malattie con le essenze delle piante*, Martello - Giunti, Firenze, 1976.

• Index •

Finito di stampare nel mese di marzo 2000
dalle Grafiche BUSTI S.r.l. - Colognola ai Colli (VR)